FROM

MENACE TO

MIRACLE

LARRY HARVEY

WITH HILARY FIELD

FROM
MENACE TO
MIRACLE

THE TRUE STORY OF HOW A
PRISONER BECAME A PRISON CHAPLAIN

From Menace to Miracle

Copyright © 2018 by Larry Harvey.

ISBN: 9781790298877

CONTENTS

ACKNOWLEDGEMENTS

I would like to thank my very good friend Hilary Field for her patience, diligence and time in helping me to write this book.

I would also like to thank Sue, not just for being my wife but also my best friend.

I would like to extend my love and gratitude to my family, who never left me when I needed them most.

And last, but not least, I thank God who was and still is my shield, my strength, my portion and my greatest help in my darkest hour.

DISCLAIMER

Gypsies/Travellers are an ethnic group and have dwelt in the UK for over five hundred years. Many fought in the Second World War and there were over five hundred thousand put to death at Auschwitz alongside six million Jews. Gypsies/Travellers are still victims of racism in the 21st Century. As with every race, creed or colour there may be a small minority of Gypsies/Travellers that give the rest a bad name. Racist words include 'gyppo', 'pikey' and 'tinker' to name a few.

I do not want to imply in telling my story that all Gypsies/Travellers end up as prisoners, any more than I want to imply that all prisoners end up as prison chaplains.

Chapter 1

THE 'GYPPO' KID

'Mum, am I really dirty?'

I peered up at my mum, a frown on my face and tears in my eyes.

'Of course you're not Larry,' she said indignantly. 'Your clothes are all brand new and you're the smartest little boy in the school.'

But when you're the one who's different, when your mum and dad live on their own land in a caravan in the country, and your family is known to everyone around as 'those gyppos', being the best dressed child in the local infant school isn't any help. You're a Gypsy and Gypsies are there to be hated.

I was 5 years old when the taunts began. I'd gone off to school with high hopes, but returned home to my parents' land in north Bristol a changed little boy. From that day on I hated school.

My mum and dad, brother-in-law and big sister all took it in turns to take me to school every day, with me struggling and screaming at them, 'I'm not going!' I often wouldn't stay and if I did, I kicked up a fuss. I was always being told to stand outside the headmistress's room by the big fish tank and wait to be punished. One day, the punishment went too far when the headmistress slapped me so hard on my little legs I went home with a big red mark showing up below my shorts. Mum was furious and marched down to the school to complain. But nothing changed.

I did try very hard. I was so desperate to fit in. When the school band started I was really excited and begged to be able to hit the big drum. But I never did get to play it. I was given the triangle instead. It was a big disappointment and a humiliation and it only added to my resentment and hatred of being 'different'.

Primary school has mainly bad memories for me, but there were a few happy times too. One day my whole class were allowed to troop outside to sit under a tree in the hot summer sun and listen to our teacher read us a story. I loved that. I loved being outside and I enjoyed the stories from the *Ladybird Books*, especially the ones about birds. I was in my element. This was what I was used to, being outside in the fresh air amongst birds and nature. When I was shut up in the classroom, I used to look out through the window to try and see the birds that I had read about in my books. The hours used to drag by. The best time of all was when my mum came to meet me to drive me home each day.

Things still didn't improve when I transferred to the Junior School. All my brothers and sister received the same treatment. There were a couple of nice teachers though and I never forgot them. There was kind, lovely Miss SP. She seemed to be one of the few people trying to understand and help me. There was also Mrs Hoskins, who was one of the few able to keep me in line, but at the same time she was very kind and caring. My frustration and loneliness came out in moments of bad temper and after one of my outbursts Miss SP told me, 'Look Larry, if you're going to lose your temper, hit a tree or something, not a person.' It's one of the few times in my school days someone tried to help me, instead of telling me off and making me feel worse.

I had such a dislike for school that I spent a lot of my childhood at home with my mum and dad. They were busy demolishing two old cottages on their land. Dad was building a brand-new bungalow where the cottages had been. When it was finished we all moved in and lived there as a family. We were living in much better style than most of our neighbours and still had caravans in our backyard.

But I was mischevious even then. When I was around 8 years old my brother Pete and I used to take tools from dad's scrapyard and cut through the chicken wire surrounding our neighbour's hedge so we could pick apples from the orchard.

Dad was a scrap metal merchant and a very successful one. He drove a Rolls-Royce Silver Shadow and my mum had her own car too; unheard of in those days, especially in rural north Bristol. From the bungalow windows, we looked out over acres of beautiful countryside. I loved that almost as much as I loved our animals. The Harvey family animals were a big part of our lives. We once had a goat which had been mistreated by others before it had been given to me and when it had to be put down, I was heartbroken. Then my dad bought a donkey called Ted, to replace the goat. There were also two cats, Tom Jones and Elvis, who sat happily washing themselves in the sunshine. All of this, surrounded by silky bunny rabbits and contented chickens clucking in the yard.

Ted the donkey was a terror though. Dad and I could often be seen running around the field trying to catch him. He was stubborn and promptly sat down the minute he was saddled up for riding and wouldn't budge. Nothing we did could get him to go! In the end, we would have to unsaddle him and watch him wander happily off into the distance, cropping the grass as he went. At other times, I would be hugging the baby bunnies or chatting to Blackie, our Border Collie Labrador cross. Blackie happily followed me through the fields on our many adventures. There were cattle in the meadows at one point too. My dad had bought them with plans to sell them on as beef, but when it came to it he couldn't bring himself to send them to market to be killed, so they stayed and joined the ever-growing family, as we all lived the 'good life' together.

Horses also played a big part in our family way of life, as they do for all true Gypsies. I was lucky enough to have my own horse called Bonnie, a strawberry roan. I loved riding her around dad's fields. I also discovered a kind of school which I actually liked; the Henfield Riding School, where I went to learn how to ride. It cost 50p an hour and I loved every minute of it. There were other stables too, right opposite where I lived at Mrs Bird's house, and I loved to hang out there as well. I joked and laughed with the stable boys and girls and we rode the horses for miles in the summer. They were some of the happiest times of my life and it was there I met a young boy, John Benjamin, who was to become my friend for life.

Whenever I returned home, tired and hungry, my mum was there, loving and caring for me and my three brothers and sister. My mother was a full-blooded Gypsy and proud of it: she had grown up in the old ways. She had lived in a Gypsy wagon with her mother and seven brothers and sisters, travelling from place to place. The seasons dictated where and how they lived. When it was summer, they went pea-picking. In winter, it was time for buying and selling rags, scrap and horse manure on the streets of Bristol. It had been a hard but happy childhood for my mother. Through all her travels, she never had the opportunity to learn to read and write. This made her determined that her five children should get the opportunity she never had. She was a lovely mum, kind and hardworking. She always made sure the caravan was scrubbed clean, she mended all our clothes and cooked huge family dinners on the stove.

I remember her own mother, Alice Ayres, my gran. She was a small but very strong-willed woman. She had had to be! She'd grown up in an old horse-drawn wagon, married young, been widowed early and was left to bring up her eight children on her own, as she travelled and lived in the wagon. She never let them down and always made sure they had enough to eat, ending each day in a safe place along the road. At that time, a safe night stop was getting increasingly difficult to find with council laws making more and more restrictions on where Gypsies could and couldn't stay for the night. But she always found somewhere.

Summer was the best time of all for us. With it came seasonal pea-picking, swede-pulling and hop-picking. We travelled from farm to farm, met old friends from last season and after a hard day sat round the fire in the evenings, telling stories and reminiscing.

This seasonal work continued right through my childhood. I loved it and was a little daredevil. My poor mum was always having to take me to hospital to be patched up.

When I was just 2 years old, I was playing near my mother who was pea-picking and I managed to run into the heavy bird scarer so hard that it fell and hit me in the face. The bird scarer was almost impossible to move and my cousin told my mum that he had never known anyone so young to be so strong. Even as a baby I once rocked my pram so hard that it broke apart and my parents had to put weights in my playpen because I could drag it with me wherever I crawled.

Aged 5 I was playing in the fields as usual while my mum was busy pea-picking, when I ran across the lane to look at a big tractor in the fields opposite. Excited by what I'd seen, I dashed back to tell my mum. As I did so, I wasn't looking where I was going and I was hit by a car head on. I remember being tossed up into the air and landing ten feet down the road. I could hear my mum screaming and the next thing I knew I was waking up in nearby Frenchay Hospital.

And when I was 7, despite my mum and dad having already told me not to leave the driveway, I rode off up the lane on my pushbike and was hit off it by a car. Once again, I was taken to Frenchay Hospital, suffering only a few minor cuts and bruises but I found it difficult to walk properly for a few weeks, so it must have been quite bad!

Fortunately, I was none the worse for wear for this, or for the many other accidents and scrapes I got into over the coming years.

I had a softer side to me as well. I loved my mum and dad to bits and was always very affectionate towards people who were kind to me. When visitors came, I was the first to get up and help my mum collect the cups and take them back to the kitchen. I dread to think how many pieces of mum's best china got broken over the years, but she was grateful for any help she could get. When I was 8 years old, I used to sit with her and my sister making artificial flowers. Then my sister and I would try to sell them by going around knocking on neighbourhood doors.

I always had a strong will of my own and as a young boy I particularly hated going to the dentist. One day my mum took me and my brother Pete along for a check-up and Pete went in to see the dentist first. I watched in horror as he came out of the room crying, with blood coming from his mouth. There was nothing else for it, I had to escape, so I got out of my chair and made for the door, wrenched it open and ran down the street as fast as my little legs could carry me, followed by my mum, the dentist and the nurse, all chasing and calling after me down the high street.

As time went on, my older brothers and sister got married one by one. Some went to live in their own caravans on dad's land but my older sister, whom I was really close to, moved away to Bridgwater. I missed her. One week, she surprised us all by coming back to visit. I was sitting on the bungalow steps when I looked up and saw her walking down the path. I was thrilled. I stood up, disappeared into the bungalow and came out wearing my wellington boots, with a little bag all packed and ready to go back with her. But it didn't work. I wasn't allowed to go and had to stay to face the school I hated so much.

All this time, while I was growing up, I was learning lessons; some good and some bad. I learned that to be a Gypsy meant that lots of adults and children don't like you. People will say mean things to you and won't let you play with them, however much you want them to. I also learned that if you stood up to the bullies (and there were plenty of them) and fought furiously with them, they wouldn't bother you anymore. This particular lesson would get me into a lot of trouble when I was older. But I did grow up to have many close friends from my area of Blackhorse.

I also learned a softer side to life; my mum and my gran were both caring and gentle. My gran taught me something that stayed with me through all the hard times and the good. She came to stay with us every now and then and as I lay awake on my bed at night, I would hear her saying her prayers.

Curious, I looked up at her one day and asked, 'What are you doing Gran?'

She smiled down at me, 'I'm praying to God, Larry. For you and for all of our family. I pray every night.'

When she came to stay, I always liked hearing her stories of the old days. I was very sad when she passed away. I was 10 years old. She had a traditional Gypsy funeral, with over five hundred people from the Gypsy world across the country attending and a cortège of twenty shiny black cars. Her passing left me feeling sad and quite lost, but she had left me with a lifelong legacy. From then on, I followed my gran's example and I said my prayers every night, even when things were so black in my life that I felt like there was no hope. I always said my prayers.

School continued and one particular term my class had to go to another school for a few months as our old classroom was being rebuilt. At that time, there were two bullies who continuously picked on a select few of the children and it wasn't long before it was my turn. Eventually, it reached the stage where I had had enough, so I hit the two of them - and they never bothered with me again.

When I wasn't beating off the bullies, there were a few happy times, especially at secondary school, when the bullying stopped. All of these happy times had one thing in common for me; they were connected with being allowed outside. This was where I was most at home and could use my love of nature and the outdoors. Because most of it was outdoors, I worked enthusiastically on my Duke of Edinburgh Award Scheme and got as far as gaining the Bronze and Silver Medals. I loved camping in the fields with my two friends and building fires to cook our tea. I loved playing rugby at school and was good enough to be picked for the school team. When I wasn't playing rugby, one of my teachers, Mr Bishop, allowed me to work in the garden outside instead of doing some of his lessons. That suited me much better than being cooped up in a stuffy classroom. Mr Bishop was a teacher who won my respect by being very strict but incredibly kind.

Things took an even better turn when my dad introduced me and my younger brother to boxing. When I was around 13, my dad took Pete and I off to the local boxing club. It was the best thing he could have done. We really enjoyed it. Both of us went into the Schoolboy and Junior Championships and continued boxing for many years afterwards. We made many lifelong friends at the Empire Boxing Club in Bristol. This sport led me into lots of adventures over the years, both good and bad and some I would never want to live through again!

Chapter 2

A TALENT FOR BOXING

'It'll knock some sense into you,' my dad said.

He was explaining why he was taking me to a boxing club. I was such a restless child, always looking for something to stop the boredom. The trouble was, I often chose the wrong thing to replace it.

My parents' worst fears came true when I was finally accused of a serious offence. Stealing. I was just 12 years old. I had broken into my Junior School on a Saturday night with a couple of friends to steal money out of the headmaster's office, but mainly for the sheer thrill of it. It had been my idea and I thought we had got away with it until a policeman called round to the caravan on the Sunday and asked to see me. My parents were devastated. I was questioned and found guilty. My punishment was to be made to attend a YMCA (Young Men's Christian Association) centre every Saturday for several hours to do physical education, which I hated. My mum and dad were not best pleased either so they grounded me as well. It was not a happy time, but none of that stopped me.

One night I had a few mates come over to the house when my mum and dad were out for the evening. I took the key to my mum's new van and began to drive it up and down the lane.

One of the lads wanted to drive.

'OK,' I said. 'But take it steady.'

He didn't heed my advice and drove too fast and ended up hitting a telegraph pole, hard. I hit the windscreen and cut both my hands. I really needed stitches but I would not go to hospital. I ran back home and asked my brother George and his mates to tow the van back home. It was a total write-off. I was so scared that I ran away from home, only to ring my mum and dad later to say sorry. They were more concerned about me and if I was OK, rather than the van, so I came back home, tail between my legs.

Something inside me made me continue doing stupid and foolhardy things and I went from borrowing my mum's car to stealing other people's. I crept about in the night, and sometimes in the daytime too. I used scrap keys to open the vehicles and drove them around, aged 12, through the streets. It gave me a thrill, until one day there was a thrill too many.

I was out at nine o'clock at night, clinging on to the passenger seat with my mate driving, and four others in the back seat when our car narrowly missed two girls on the pavement who were out walking their dog. In order to miss the two girls, my friend swerved and we drove straight into a stone wall. I went flying through the windscreen and landed on the bonnet. I don't remember anything until I was arrested a couple of miles down the road, covered in blood and trying to stagger home on foot. This time I was sent to Juvenile Court, received a fine and was put under a supervision order with a probation officer who did me no favours.

My dad didn't want this to happen again. He decided it was time to act, which is why he took me and Pete to the Empire

Boxing Club.

'This will fill your time better than getting into trouble on the streets,' he said. 'And it will teach you how to handle yourselves if you do get into trouble.'

As far as I was concerned, it was the best thing my dad could have done. From the first minute I entered the ring, I fell in love with boxing.

Over the next few months, boxing became a way of life for me. It was something that crossed every barrier of class, religion and colour; the gym was a melting pot of all three. With boxing gloves on and rules to obey, everyone from all walks of life, different faiths and nationalities were on good fighting terms.

In the gym I learned to obey the rules and enjoy the discipline of a sport that allowed me to let off steam without really hurting anybody. I remember speaking to my brother-in-law Henry, nicknamed 'Scutty', the day after winning my first boxing contest. Scutty had given me a hearty, 'Well done.' This was the last time I spoke to him before he died, leaving my sister Kathy with four children when she was just 26 years old. That dealt a big blow to the family. We were all heartbroken.

I showed a real talent for boxing and with the help of Alan Thompson and Billy Walker, boxing trainers, I entered all the Saturday night contests. I wanted to win. That's all I thought about, winning, and I usually did. I fought my way up through the ranks of the Junior Boxing Championship. My dad was so proud of me and I was proud of myself and excited with what I had achieved. It gave me a great feeling to know that I was in amongst the top of my league in a sport that was tough and challenging.

I took advantage of my talent to win the odd prize money.

Travelling fairs came to town every so often and they had their own boxing rings where professional boxers would take on members of the public for money. The public were usually soundly beaten, but I often won.

I also fought on the same bill as fellow boxer Chris Sanigar, who went on to be a successful boxing promoter and put boxing on the map in the South West. One time we travelled together on the ferry to The Channel Islands for a West Country v. Channel Islands competition. I just about recovered from a horrible bout of seasickness that night, in order to fight! It was touch and go, but we did it!

With my boxing success, my Duke of Edinburgh awards and playing in the school rugby team, I was on a winning streak as far as sport was concerned. But it wasn't the same outside the boxing ring.

In the difficult world of school and in our neighbourhood, I believed rules were there to be broken and so I did just that. Outside of the boxing club I was wild and headstrong. From being recognized for my sporting abilities, I became recognized mainly for fighting in the playground. Most fights ended with the headmaster's cane giving me six of the best. As painful as this punishment was, I often got the better of the master by putting a book down the back of my trousers to take the edge off the sting.

Away from the ring, I kicked up against what I saw as unnecessary restrictions at school and the prejudiced attitudes of the people around me and my family. Fighting and scrapping became the norm. Other habits kicked in early too; I started taking cannabis when I was 14 and I continued to steal cars at the rate of two or three a week, abandoning them in the middle of nowhere when me and my friends had had our fun. I never gave a thought to the trouble I was causing for the car owners and their families, who would wake up to find no car in the morning and no way of getting to work, or to the hospital or to visit sick relatives.

Maybe because of my devil-may-care attitude, I was a bit of a hit with the girls. I started to go out with my first girlfriend at the stables when I was just 10 years old and I was never short of a girl, often more than one, from that day on. Some girls loved me, while others thought I was OK, but different. With my wild streak, girls seemed to find me attractive, and I definitely wasn't complaining.

School had some good points, but not enough to keep me out of trouble. A place of discipline and rules, being shut in a classroom didn't give a boy like me a chance to learn. I was too much of an individual to fit in. My life outside the classroom was so different from the other boys and girls I went to school with. No one understood where I was coming from.

Growing up, I had lived an outdoor and independent life, with a love of animals and a love of freedom. I could top my schoolmates and teachers' academic knowledge hands down with my knowledge of horses and the secrets of the countryside. Unfortunately, that sort of knowledge wasn't valued by the education system.

If my unique way of life had been understood and they had found the right way for me to learn, I could have taken a different path in life and perhaps even been at the top of the academic league; a reality which I was able to prove much later in life. One or two of my teachers did try to help me. I could see that my French teacher and a few others who had the compassion and wisdom to see beyond my troubled character to the real me, were on my side.

Despite these kind teachers, I still felt I was 'classed as nothing' in school. It was a terrible feeling, so I made up for it with fights and battles and that became my way of life. Like a lot of young people with no real hope and with low self-esteem, rebelling and escaping from my troubles was all I cared about. I began to smoke marijuana and drink alcohol with my friends in the evenings and during the many days when I played hooky from school. It wasn't surprising that, after a while, this led me into deep trouble and endless fights; fights definitely not fought within the boundaries of the rules of the boxing club.

Alcohol played a big part in my world from when I was very young. When I was 9 I got so drunk at my brother's wedding that my older brother had to take me home. My mum and dad were upset by the sight of me out of my head and sick from alcohol. Nevertheless, that didn't stop me. The next year, aged 10, I headed to The Folly Pub up the road from my home and had my first pint in a bar. My 14-year-old mate went and bought it for me. I dropped that first pint, so wasn't off to a good start, but when the laughter had died down, I soon had another, and another and another. At family parties I would snaffle a few drinks when no one was looking. A few years later, in one particular local pub, someone had told the landlord and landlady that I was only 16. Of course, I had told them I was definitely 18. To which the landlord had replied, 'Bring in your birth certificate Larry and I'll serve you if what you say is true.' Not to be outdone, I took advice from a friend and managed to alter my birth certificate to show my age as being 18. The landlord was most surprised but very apologetic.

Because I started drinking underage in the local pub, I learned other ways to avoid getting caught. There used to be a police inspector who came regularly into pubs to catch out landlords who served underage drinkers and to catch the drinkers themselves. Dodging this inspector became a popular game for me. I had my pint of beer with me but next to my beer, I always had a bottle of Coke. The moment the inspector appeared, I would ignore the beer and pick up the Coke. This went on for years until one day, the inspector came in and I accidentally ignored the Coke and drank the beer instead. The inspector was thrilled to have caught me at last.

He grinned, 'Larry, I'll have you for drinking.'

'No you won't. Hard luck, I'm 18 today!' I called out across the bar. He left to the sound of the whole pub cheering and laughing. Poor bloke!

Drinking underage had its problems. It inevitably led to fights in the pubs. These fights could be started over nothing at all.

Like the time I turned to a bloke sitting next to me who was staring. 'Alright?' I asked.

'No, not really,' he grunted.

'Why not?'

'I don't want to give you an answer.'

With that, he stood up, all 6 foot 3 of him, and grabbed me by the arms. I held onto him and then this giant of a man let me go and lurched towards the door. *"Thank goodness for that. He's going"*, I thought. No such luck. Instead, he turned around, grabbed the microphone stand at the edge of the stage, ran back towards me and tried to hit me on the head with it. The fight that followed was bad enough for the landlord to have to call the Riot Squad. All hell broke loose. When the police arrived, the fighting had stopped and they couldn't prove who was involved. That was a lucky escape, in more ways than one.

I may not have studied much at school, but I had managed to

learn great survival techniques in the dangerous world I mixed in outside of school. These techniques were not so good that they always kept me out of harm's way or terrible trouble.

One evening, when I was 15, I was down the town with my mates and we decided to go to the Unigate Club, which had a disco upstairs. A bit of a scrap started in the toilets. A few of us got involved and we ended up outside, waiting for a taxi or a bus to take us home. As we waited, the blokes we had fought with in the toilets appeared. One of them was a massive man, he must have been 6 foot 5. He came towards us, along with a few of the other blokes we had been fighting. It turned out, the one I had been fighting with had lost his gold chain and this bloke was asking where the chain was. I didn't have it. He punched my mate against a window. I ran down the road, found a steel bar and hid in a shop doorway.

'Oi!' I shouted down the street, 'Come on then, see what you can do with me.'

He started running towards me and when he was just close enough, I leapt out of the doorway and struck him across the arms with the steel bar. I thought that would stop him, but it didn't. To my horror, he carried on and chased me for miles.

My mate Martin called out after him. 'Leave him alone, he's only 15!'

At which point, he head-butted Martin, who fell to the ground, and continued to chase me for another half a mile up the road. In the end, I managed to escape, but things like that were always happening to me and if I'm honest, I loved it!

But the odds were stacking up against me.

Time in a physical activity centre, probation.... what would be next?

Chapter 3

A SHORT, SHARP, SHOCK

The way I was carrying on, everyone knew I'd get into serious trouble sooner or later, including me. I always had the feeling I would go to prison for a long time, but there were a lot of scraps to come before that would happen.

Such as the time I went to The Grand Hotel in Bristol to drink. I was 15 years old. The doorman took one look at me and said, 'You've got jeans on,' and threw me out, giving me a push. As he pushed me, I hit my head hard on the scaffolding which was around the door. My head started to bleed badly. With blood pouring down my face, I lost my temper. I took off my belt, struggling with the buckle because I'd only got one good hand that day (I'd sprained the left one playing rugby for school that morning) and hit the doorman smack in the face with the belt. By that time, another security guard had come to the rescue and I hit him hard on the shoulder, so hard that he fell to the ground.

I guessed by this time that the police would be there any minute, so I took off down the road and joined a queue of people outside a nearby nightclub. But the dripping blood gave me away and I was picked out and arrested in the queue. They took me to Bridewell Police Station, in the centre of Bristol, and kept me in all night. In the morning, my mum and dad were called to come and take me home. They weren't too happy about it but I was convinced that I had been treated unfairly and told them it wasn't my fault.

The case went to Bristol Juvenile Court in November 1977. The prosecutor read out the doorman's statement which didn't match my version of what happened at all. The doorman was informed that I was only 15, but this didn't endear him to forgive me. Instead, he advised the court to 'throw the key away and never let him out.' Fortunately, the magistrate didn't agree completely, but the doorman's testimony did convince her that I was the guilty party and she took the decision to give me what she called, 'a short, sharp shock'. In reality, it wasn't so short. She gave me a sentence of nine months for grievous bodily harm with intent, actual bodily harm and carrying an offensive weapon. It was a concurrent sentence, which meant I would need to serve the first one, then if I behaved myself, I would have the others hanging over me like a threat for the next year if I did anything wrong again.

When the policeman standing next to me in the dock put the handcuffs on me to lead me away, my mum broke down and collapsed. Only years later did I realize what an effect my actions had had on my poor mum. At the time I was upset as well, but for myself, as well as for my mum and dad. I was also in a state of shock and frightened about what would happen. However, I toughed it out, and was taken away to spend all day in a cell in Bridewell. That evening, I was taken to a juvenile detention centre near Gloucester called Eastwood Park. The police officers told me if I behaved myself I would be alright, but I was to find out the police officers were wrong.

I was nervous and secretly worried about what would happen to me but I was determined not to show it, so I brazened it out, got out of the police car and walked into the centre.

I tried to be respectful when I arrived, took my compulsory shower, put on my prison clothes and was going quietly into my cell. Within minutes, I was to see what life was going to be like at Eastwood Park. I was taken to see the governor where I was punched and kicked right in front of him by an Irish officer, for not standing up properly. What the Irish officer hadn't told the governor was that he had hit me hard in the stomach *before* he brought me to see the governor, so I couldn't stand up straight even if I wanted to. This wasn't the only time it happened. Despite behaving well in a desperate attempt to avoid the beatings, I was punched and kicked every day after that for the first three weeks I was in prison. In between the beatings, I was so worried I felt sick. The trauma of it stays with me to this day.

Things have changed a lot now, with more protection for the lads in prison and more understanding and restrained behaviour by prison officers, but in those days there were hardly any checks on how inmates were treated. I reckon it was at its worst when I was there.

There were crazy rules too, made to be broken, of course. We were given just two minutes to shower, shave and use the toilet every morning. Anyone who wasn't able to manage all of that in the two minutes - and believe me you never could - was smacked in the mouth and they didn't only use their fists to hit us.

In the first week, I was made to clean the toilets and the floors. One day there was an incident in the gym. I remember it was a boy who had broken wind. We thought it was funny, but an officer known as 'Babyface' decided to hit every boy in the gym across the backside with a cricket bat, because no one would own up who did it. The next day, my parents came to see me and I was in such pain that I couldn't sit down to talk to them.

'What happened?' they asked.

'Nothing.'

I wouldn't tell them. I was worried about the hidings I would get if I told.

It seems almost impossible to imagine now but back then that kind of treatment was the norm. No kindness, no discussion, no reasoning, no thought as to what had brought us to where we were, and certainly no constructive help to get us back to a normal life.

That same officer who hit me with a cricket bat was also very impressed by money and a show of wealth. One day, he was standing looking out of the window and I was behind him on my hands and knees cleaning floors. As he looked out, he saw a Silver Shadow Rolls-Royce turn into the detention centre car park and whistled in admiration. 'That's my mum and dad,' I said, standing up to look through the window with him. From that day on that officer was a different man. When Christmas came he made all the other boys take their cards down until Christmas Day, yelling, 'It's not Christmas yet,' but he left mine hanging up. The Silver Shadow Rolls-Royce had worked its magic!

There were more instances of cruelty and unthinking behaviour by other members of the staff too. The same Irish officer who had hit me in front of the governor, was the officer who taught guitar. This left me confused. When he taught guitar, he was quite reasonable and he seemed like a different person, but I wasn't able to relax. The whole time I felt like hitting him back but I couldn't because I knew that if I did, I would never get out of there. Nonetheless, I kept an eye on him just in case he threw another punch.

There were a few bright spots amongst the gloom. One day the Annual Prison Weightlifting Competition was announced. It was to be put on by the Weightlifting Section of the Empire Sports Club and boys from other clubs would come into the prison to compete with the Eastwood Park boys. I was always fiercely competitive and, under the tuition of a staff member, I trained hard for the event, lifting weights every day in the gym every hour I was allowed.

The great day finally arrived and there was much excitement in the centre. The competitors from outside the prison were bussed in and my trainer, Billy, from the Empire Boxing Club turned up as well. I was so pleased to see him. Billy encouraged me every step of the way, which gave me a lot of extra confidence. Up until that point, any confidence I'd had in myself was being knocked out of me in the prison. The boys settled down and the fight for the Eastwood Park Trophy was on. Round after round, the boys kept cheering. The lads in Eastwood Park were cheering for me, and so were the boys from the Empire Boxing Club. I felt really popular; even more so when I won. I couldn't believe it; I'd only been training a few weeks and I was so proud of myself. When I went up to collect the trophy, the place erupted. Billy was thrilled and congratulated me. I was also congratulated by the owner of the Empire Boxing Club, Den Welch OBE, and the Welsh International Coach who was there to give the prize. It was so exciting and I felt like somebody again.

Sadly, it wasn't to last. The next day was a Sunday and I was sitting on a bench, having my lunch in the prison canteen, when the prison gym instructor who had helped to train me, came and stood in front of me.

He leaned over me and I stopped eating to look up at him.

'Harvey, well done for winning that competition,' he said. I was thrilled to have his approval. It meant so much to me.

He smiled for a moment, but then his expression changed.

'But just remember you're nothing and you'll always be nothing.'

I fought inside to stay calm and to stay on the high I had from winning but it wasn't easy. It was a shattering mental put-down from someone I had respected and who I thought had come to respect me.

Three of the teachers from my school really went the extra mile to help and encourage me. They bothered to come and visit me in the prison. To me they were a beacon of light in a dark place. I will never forget them. Mr Bishop was the metalwork teacher and was very strict but had allowed me to work outside in the school garden from time to time. Then there was Mr Young who taught English and Mr Chard, the PE teacher. They all made the effort to come separately to see me in prison and to tell me that they were thinking of me. Mr Bishop even wrote me a letter about the way my life was going and how I was better than the behaviour I was showing. That kind letter gave me encouragement which lasted for years. I began to think, 'yes, I can do better', but I just couldn't seem to settle. I would get bored very easily and always had to be doing something. I didn't break into schools and clubs for the money, it was for the excitement.

After three months into my nine-month sentence, I was released. It was just after Christmas and my mum and dad came to pick me up in the Silver Shadow Rolls-Royce. I was so excited. Out at last. Away from that place. When we got home the first thing I did was rush into my bedroom and make a beeline for my Christmas presents, which were piled up on my bed, glittering in their Christmas paper. I opened them all there and then. One of the presents was a beautiful classical guitar, which cost my parents a lot of money. I was thrilled and so proud of it.

But even the three months of bullying and rough treatment in the detention centre and the joy of coming home didn't do anything to help me turn my life around. Once my presents were opened, I couldn't wait to go out and see my mates. Within an hour of being home, I was involved in a fight at the local chip shop. It was with a guy I'd fought just before I went into prison.

The day I had gone to prison was a Monday. On the Sunday night before that, I had met this bloke in his thirties. He was wearing a Teddy Boy Suit and I said, 'That's a nice suit.'

'Ain't nothing to do with you,' was his reply and he followed it up with a punch on my lip.

My mate Martin then started a fight with him because he knew I was due in court the next day and wanted to keep me out of trouble.

The police were called and I kept quiet. My split lip didn't heal for the whole time I was in Eastwood Park, which shows how filthy the condition were in there. I remember sores came up on the cut and I thought, *'when I get out of here I'm going to get him for that'*, so when I happened to see him in the chip shop on that first night, I didn't stop to think. But then I never did, that was the trouble! I hit him and knocked him out. After which, his sister tried to stab me. The police were called and I was taken into the police station. Fortunately for me, when he woke up from his concussion, he decided not to press charges, so they let us go. I had been a bit worried at the thought of going straight back to prison I must admit, but it hadn't stopped me. Strangely enough, my opponent and I became lifelong friends after that. I went back home to spend my first night in my own bed. Safe and clean but a little the worse for wear.

The time in the detention centre still weighed heavily on my mind and I wanted to get my own back on one of the staff, a male nurse that had treated me badly. My mate owned a crossbow. He told me that the arrows could stop a charging elephant at forty yards so I asked him if he could drive me to the prison. I knew what time the nurse came in to work on his pushbike and I was going to lay in wait and try to shoot him in the knee. I now thank God that the car broke down on the way. What was I thinking?!

Around this time, as well as fighting in chip shops and lots of other places, I decided to take up boxing properly again. I went back to entering boxing contests and I did really well. In 1978, when I was 16, I went with my mum and dad to Bridgwater Fair. After trying the dodgems and going on the big wheel a few times, I went into the boxing booth. This was a tent with a boxing ring inside and chairs all around for paying spectators. Visitors to the fairground were challenged to take on the semi-professional boxer hired by the fair. If the visitor won, they got the prize money. If they lost, they left with a bloody nose and nothing else. 'Who wants to go four rounds with my boxers?' I couldn't resist the challenge. I'd always wanted to have a go in one of those booths, so I stripped off my t-shirt, stepped into the ring and faced my opponent; a big bloke with scars. It was my first paid fight and I won. In fact, I won two fights that day in the space of one hour.

I made such an impression on the boxing booth owner, that he asked me to join them as a professional fighter but I said no. All I really wanted was to go back to my life of booze, drugs and street fighting. It had a stranglehold on me. But even when I thought I was fighting fairly in the fairground, I still managed to get into trouble. With just my luck, there was a television company there that day, making a programme about Fairground Boxing Booths. Both my fights were filmed and were used in the programme that went out nationwide on television. My trainer happened to see it and he congratulated me, but added, 'You can't fight for money if you're going to continue fighting as an amateur, mate. The Amateur Boxing Federation saw it on telly and won't let you.' That was the end of my professional boxing life.

Looking back, I'm glad because I was only 16; I was interested but I was too young to stand up to constant professional fights. I would have been a wreck. Just a few years later, boxing booths were made illegal due to the fact that too many people were getting badly injured taking part in their fights. I had a lucky escape once again. My ambition at the time had been to represent my country in the 1980 Moscow Olympics, but going off the rails meant there was no chance of that.

As well as street fighting and boxing in the boxing booths, I was causing problems at football matches, fighting in the stands and after the match. I had started going to football matches around age 13, purely for the violence. I always got into scuffles and on one occasion, the opposing team surrounded the coach and tried to turn over the vehicle. That was a real fracas. I loved it, the thrill of violence. But the thrill of violence wasn't the only thing I loved and my life was about to take a different turn.

Chapter 4

RUNAWAY LOVE

The whole time I was toughing it out in the Young Offenders' Centre, I had been keeping a secret. I had met a girl and she meant more to me than all the other girls I had met before. Sue was beautiful, 5 foot 6, dark hair, 16 years old with olive skin and large dark eyes. It was love at first sight.

Sue says she remembers vividly the first time we met. She was at school and her best friend Lesley was going out with a boy called Paul. One day Lesley said to Sue, 'Paul wants to set you up with his friend, Larry. Why don't you come with me after school tonight? Larry will be outside at the gates.'

'Alright,' Sue said, but she wasn't really bothered.

We all met at the school gates, and I didn't say a word all evening. I just sat on the grassy bank outside Stockwell Hill School; I wouldn't even look at Sue. She thought I was useless! So when Lesley asked her the next day what she thought of me, Sue replied, 'Well, he's incredibly rude isn't he? He wouldn't even speak to me.' What she didn't know then was that I wasn't being rude, I was just really shy. Despite that disastrous first date, for some reason she agreed to meet up with me again. This time we met at a local golf course. I was feeling a bit more confident by then and I was a little chattier. I began telling Sue funny stories and making her laugh.

From those rocky beginnings, Sue and I began to meet more often. Gradually, she learned about my life and the things I had got up to. She didn't know I was a Gypsy and she didn't know the trouble I'd been in. When I finally told her, she was quite shocked, especially when one evening I told her, 'I need to tell you something. I'm probably going to prison soon.' Sue's first thought was, *'Oh God, I can't tell Mum and Dad'*, but it didn't put her off me. For a long time though, she didn't tell her parents that she was seeing me and when they did eventually find out, they weren't best pleased. Especially as I was her first boyfriend.

It all came to a head one night when Sue went out with me and didn't arrive back home until half past ten, when she should have been back at nine o'clock. Sue's dad was frantic and he called the police. When the policeman heard who their daughter was going out with, he recognised my name immediately and warned them not to let their daughter have anything to do with me. 'That Gypsy is bad news. He's a criminal and he can be violent. He'll lead her into trouble. He's a bad 'un.'

After that, Sue's mum and dad banned her from ever seeing me again, but we were teenagers and the ban had the opposite effect on us both. We met up in secret and decided to run away together, which was the worst thing that could have happened in Sue's parents' minds. When she didn't come home, they were distraught and they called the police once again. After a long search, Sue was found with me, living in a squat only a couple of miles down the road from her parents' house. Sue's dad persuaded her to move back home with her family but it didn't last long. Her mum's tears and her father's pleas and threats fell on deaf ears and it wasn't long before Sue came back to the squat to live with me again.

Conditions in that squat were not pleasant. It was a drug den. I started taking speed as well as other drugs and Sue smoked cannabis. The potent mixture of drugs and alcohol meant that there were plenty of fights, violence and clashes with the police. Sometimes it all got a bit much for both of us and every so often I would leave the squat to go back to my mum and dad and Sue would go back to hers. I would arrive at their place in the early hours of the morning to clean up and have a meal. I helped myself to my favourite snack, a 'Branston Sandwich', with bread, butter and pickle. My life was totally out of control but in spite of their terrible misgivings, my parents couldn't stop me from going back to the squat and getting myself into constant trouble.

Mum and Dad were always desperate to save me from myself and resorted to calling in the law to see if they could help me. It was during one of my breaks at my parents' home, that the doorbell rang. I was sleeping off a late night of drinking and drugs session and it was about nine in the morning. As I slowly woke up, I lifted my head only to see a large policeman standing in my bedroom door. I was shocked and shouted at him, 'Get out of my room!'

He grinned and said, 'Your Mum and Dad can't do anything with you, so I've come to sort you out.'

I got straight out of bed and sloped towards him.

'Do you want a fight?' I growled.

He squared up to me. 'Yeah. I do.'

With that, he jumped on top of me and we wrestled and fell onto the floor, turning over and over, arms and legs flailing.

We began hitting each other hard. I punched him in the face over and over again. With the sound of the fight, furniture crashing and me cursing, the family soon appeared. It was mayhem. My mum, dad, sister and younger brother all tried to get me off him, screaming for me to stop. There was blood everywhere. They eventually managed to pull the two of us apart, the policeman holding a handkerchief up to his bleeding nose. We stood still for a moment, glaring at each other. The tension was high. When suddenly, in the silence after the storm, my mother came out of the kitchen, teapot in hand, looked at us both and asked very politely, 'Would you like a cup of tea?' 'You give him a cup of tea and I'll ram it down his throat,' I scowled at my mother. I then turned to the policeman and growled, 'Get out of here.' He went.

Fortunately, he never pressed charges against me but about a year later we met again. Sue and I were in a crowd outside our local fish and chip shop, when about ten policemen arrived. Amongst them, was the same man who had come to my parents' home the year before to 'sort me out'. He spotted me immediately. 'Oh, here he is, mummy's boy,' he taunted and then announced to the whole crowd, 'I had to sort him out cos his Mum and Dad couldn't do anything with him.'

I walked over to him, looked him in the eyes and said loudly, 'I don't want no trouble, but look at your nose and look at mine. Who do you think won?'

It was clear that the policeman's nose had been broken, all bent and out of shape, whilst mine was the same as it had always been. With that, he said nothing, turned around and got back into his car and drove away to the sound of the laughing crowd.

Meanwhile, life at the squat continued to be a mishmash of all-night drinking, taking drugs, fighting and crime. One night I went out to buy more cannabis. My mate lent me his bike to get hold of some drugs and I and another friend revved the 850cc motorbike down the M32 towards Bristol centre, breaking the speed limit with ease. When the police tagged onto us and tried to get us to stop, I swerved dangerously near the railings. The blue lights were flashing behind us and the sirens were wailing but I wouldn't stop. The police gave chase and I drove the bike across a motorway bridge. Then I decided, in my drug-fuelled state, to jump off the bike and off the bridge. I pulled the bike to a stop, turned to my mate and yelled, 'I'm gonna jump!' I sprung up off the bike, ran to the barrier and jumped. It was a long way down to the grass verge below and I was knocked out for a split second. I came round, got up off the grass and promptly legged it to a nearby park. By this time the police had called for reinforcements and had dogs. I could hear the sound of the chase and the barking behind me, so I headed for the park lake and waded in, my heavy coat pulling me under as I tried to escape.

I managed to wade a few yards against the water to the other side and stayed in the lake, huddled against the bank, listening to the dogs as they searched for me. A couple of hours later, when the noise had died down, I pulled myself out onto the bank. I had shaken them off, the police were nowhere to be seen and I squelched my way up to a phone box, called a taxi and gave the address of my squat. The taxi driver asked me why I was so wet and I passed it off by telling him someone had chucked a couple of pints of beer over me. The next day, my friend returned to pick up his motorbike and found it chained to the railings. When he went to have it unlocked, he told the police he didn't know who had stolen it. They weren't able to prove otherwise, so they couldn't do anything about it. Yet another near escape from the law for me.

A few weeks later, myself and my mate from the squat were desperate for fags and broke into a shop, stole some cigarettes and lighters and left through the window, leaving it open as we went. The police suspected it was someone from the squat and came looking for evidence. I was arrested when they found the cigarettes and a lighter from the shop in my room. My poor, long-suffering mother came with me to see a solicitor. 'It's not looking very good Mrs Harvey,' she told us. However, luck was on my side that day and the case was thrown out of court on a technicality; my mum had not been present at the police interview and I was under age so should not have been interrogated on my own. Back to the squat I went, free once more.

Sue and I stayed at the squat for twelve months. By that time, Sue was working in an office, holding down a job, but her lifestyle caught up with her. She was getting up early every morning to go to work and trying to lead an ordinary life during the day, then she stayed up drinking, partying and getting into trouble all through the night and it eventually took its toll on her. Not surprisingly, she lost her job. I continued to deal in cannabis and work for my dad at the scrap metal yard, driving vans around the area collecting scrap. It was hard, physical work but I was strong and in spite of my drug-taking and erratic lifestyle, I kept up with the work. I loved being with my dad and life at the scrapyard was good, unlike life at the squat.

By this time, my friends were leaving the area and I was in constant trouble from the company I was keeping. In fact, out of the ten of us who lived in the squat only three, including myself and Sue, have managed to live past the age of 40. Drugs and alcohol took their lives. It was a life filled with constant excitement and stress. There was a time that I had planned to rob a local bank using my father's shotgun, but once again I thank God that my dad had hidden the gun and I couldn't find it.

Everyone who lived in the squat was in some kind of trouble.

Two of the men in the squat were on the run from the police and I got talking to them one day.

'We're going for a car,' one of them said.

'To steal?' I asked.

'Yeah.'

'And a grandfather clock,' the other piped up.

Sue decided to tag along too, out of loyalty to me.

We stole the car and on the way to collect the grandfather clock, we broke into a warehouse through a back window, but in doing so we triggered the warehouse alarm. We scrambled out through the window and ran back to the car, gunning it down the road to try to get away. It was too much for the car and a few miles down the road it overheated and ground to a halt. By this time, we were so hyped up, we decided to break into another car, but the minute we opened the doors, the car alarm started to screech. We got out as quickly as we could and all ran down the road. Unsurprisingly, the car alarm had alerted some neighbours and two policemen to our presence and they started to chase after us.

Sue was terrified. *'What have I got myself into? I can't do this.... what will my Dad think? I'm never ever doing this again'*, she gasped as she hurtled down the road with me and my mates.

The police were on foot and began to chase us. We all legged it. We jumped over some railings into a playground and from there managed to climb up onto a school roof. But one of the policemen was as fast as us and he grabbed the end of my shirt and used it to haul himself up. I managed to pull off the shirt and wriggle free. I continued to run across the roof until I looked back and spotted Sue. She had lost a shoe and had sprained her ankle. I watched as the second policeman rugby tackled and wrestled her to the ground. I was sweating and panting. I had been ready to run again but I changed my mind and yelled to my two mates, telling them that I wasn't going back to the squat. Instead, I stopped, turned to the police and called out, 'I'm surrendering cos you've got my girlfriend.' The police hauled us both off to the station.

Once in the police station, a policeman began to push Sue

around. She was terrified and I wasn't going to allow that.

I faced the policeman.

'Do you want a fight?'

'Yeah,' he said.

He led me into a cell but the fight never happened. He slammed the cell door and locked me in. Sue was put in a cell by herself; it was the darkest, dampest cell you could ever imagine. There was water running down the walls. It was like a dungeon. While she was there, something happened which added to her terror. She was strip-searched. She later told me about her ordeal.

'I have never felt so humiliated in my life. It was horrible.'

The Criminal Investigation Department (CID) eventually arrived and Sue and I were accused of armed robbery. This was a shock, as it wasn't true and it was a much more serious charge than breaking and entering. After a couple of phone calls, we were allowed out on bail and were charged with riding in a stolen car. We went to court where I was fined £80 and Sue was fined £10.

In my usual fashion, I didn't care and I liked the violence more than the breaking and entering. I liked the feeling it gave me. Sue did care, she never got her shoe back and she never came out with me again on one of my escapades.

Chapter 5

ALWAYS UP FOR A FIGHT

Our family often visited us whilst we were living in the squat. One night Sue's father and my mother came to the squat together in an attempt to persuade us to come home. We agreed to go back and Sue's father and mother arranged a meeting with myself and Sue at the local pub. They wanted to have a friendly chat to try and get along with the boyfriend who had taken their daughter away from them. The meeting was better than anyone could have hoped and resulted in a truce, which lasted for a short while. However, I was not the sort of man who popped over for afternoon tea, or went out for a quiet family meal. Something always happened to cut through the peace. The truce did not last.

On Sue's eighteenth birthday, it was arranged that the whole family, including me, would go out to a local hotel for a birthday meal and a drink. Sue was excited. The meal was booked in advance and she had told me that I was to wear something nice and be there for 7.30 p.m. That evening, when I didn't show up, Sue was heartbroken. Her mum and dad were upset for her too. Sometime after this I made contact with Sue. I told her that I was sorry I hadn't gone to her birthday and explained it was because I was embarrassed and didn't feel comfortable with the idea of sitting with her whole family. Sue forgave me and we started to see each other again, but her dad was not happy about this at all.

After a short while Sue left home again and returned with me to the squat. We lived there until one night we met my older brother George in the pub and agreed to go and live with him, his wife Pauline and their baby. The new home was a world away from the dirty squat with its all night music and constant cannabis smoking.

There was only one reason we agreed to move and it was a big one; Sue was pregnant. We moved out of the squat and into George and Pauline's home where things were much more comfortable. It was clean for a start, with a proper bathroom and running water. No more climbing out of windows to escape the police, at least not for Sue.

My life continued on its wild course. The expected baby didn't change a thing for me. I was willing to try anything that could get me high, including whatever nature could offer. One day I heard that there were magic mushrooms in a field nearby, so myself and a friend caught a bus to go and have a look. The rumours were true; we discovered some unusual looking mushrooms growing in a field which had a 'no public right of way' sign. Ignoring it, we picked as many as we could that day. A week later, I wanted to go back but when it came to it, my mate wouldn't come with me. I decided to catch a bus and go on my own, just as it was getting dark.

I got off the bus, climbed over the fence and began picking what I could see through the gloom. Never one to wait for anything, I started eating the mushrooms there and then, and as darkness fell, began to light matches in order to see the mushrooms in, what was now, total darkness. The mushrooms were indeed 'magic'. They definitely had an effect on me. Full up and completely out of my head, I climbed back over the fence and swayed down the road, sticking my thumb out for a lift back to town. The last bus had gone.

After about an hour, a little old Morris Minor 1000 pulled up beside me and its driver offered me a lift home. Inside, were three middle-aged women. I climbed gratefully into the back seat. Half out of my mind, I was sitting back in the seat with my eyes closed when I felt a long, wet tongue slowly exploring my ear. *'This is nice'*, I thought and I got ready to give the woman my best smile. As I turned around, through my mushroom haze, I could see a gorgeous lady dressed only in an expensive Afghan coat. But when the mist of the magic mushrooms cleared a little, I sat bolt upright as I realized the "lady" was a very large, hairy Afghan hound, lovingly caressing my face. I screamed, 'Stop the car, stop the car!' The women were surprised, the car screeched to a halt and I shot out of the back seat and onto the road. I walked the rest of the way home. I never returned to the field and the three middle-aged women and the Afghan hound were never seen again.

A few weeks later, I had been at a funeral drinking with friends all day and we decided to go on to a club. Inside the club, the music was loud, it was dark and I was very drunk. I saw one of my mates fighting a doorman who had said something to him he didn't like. I pitched in and took on a second doorman. The next thing we knew, the crowd was against us, we were punched and kicked all the way through the club and thrown outside. I lost consciousness, but when I came to, I saw that one of the doormen was still hitting my mate. I felt very ill and called out, 'Let him alone and we'll go.' Which we did, disaster averted.

The next day, after I had sobered up, I realized I had lost my mum's precious gold chain which I had been wearing that day. I was horrified. My mum loved that gold chain. I had to go back to the club to find it. The landlord opened the door, took one look at me and said, 'I heard there was trouble last night and if you want more trouble, I've got some mates I can call.'

That was like a red rag to a bull to me. I was always up for a fight. 'Well go and get them then,' I challenged, squaring up to him.

A short while later, a car arrived with four big lads inside and they looked like they were ready for a fight. But instead of teaching me a lesson on behalf of the landlord, they got out of the car, walked up to me, clapped me on the back and said, 'Hey Larry, what's the problem?' The landlord stood open-mouthed. I told them why I was there, 'I just came back for me Mum's gold chain.' The boys helped me look inside the club but we never did find it. I was embarrassed when I had to tell my mum I'd lost it but at least a fight had been avoided.

My friends always supported me, but family ties were even stronger in times of trouble. The Harvey's stuck together through thick and thin. It was us against the rest of the world. No matter what it took; when Sue and I went with my mum and dad to Cadbury Heath Social Club to meet my aunt and uncle, we weren't expecting any trouble. It was just a family outing. We usually had a good time in the club, but not this time.

Sue and I were waiting outside for my mum and dad when a man we didn't know came out with a lad around the age of 14 and dragged the youngster by his arm down an alleyway. I thought he was going to hit him and Sue and I were worried for the boy. I called out to him something not very complimentary. The man turned around and immediately punched me in the face (I was eating a ham roll at the time) and made me choke. I hit him back and Sue screamed. The sound brought the bloke's brothers and father out of the club, who took one look at the scene and started hitting and kicking me and I went down.

Sue was terrified. She thought they were going to kill me. They were big men and meant business but Sue, who was seven months pregnant at the time, didn't hesitate. She rushed in to defend me, jumping on the man's back and screaming for help. My aunt, mother and father all came out of the club and promptly dived into the fray. One of the men hit my aunt and she fell to the floor, so I immediately hit him back. Then someone else picked on my mum, who was on crutches at the time. These boys hadn't reckoned with the Harvey fighting spirit and my mum promptly whacked him over the head with her crutch and then knocked another of them out cold. The furore meant that the police soon arrived at the scene. Just before we heard the sirens, I ran up to the biggest bloke and shouted, 'I blame you!' I knocked him out and left him on the ground. The fight ceased and everyone scattered. No one was caught by the police.

After recovering overnight, I went back the next day with my brothers to the club to find my coat. It was my favourite velvet jacket. I eventually found it in the yard outside the club. The only trouble was, half of it was at the front of the club and the other half was round the back. That's how fierce the fighting had been. My brothers wanted revenge on the other family. They tried to find out where they'd gone but word on the street was that they were in hiding, lying low until the heat died down. It was all just part and parcel of life as we knew it. We never saw them again.

Chapter 6

NEW BABY

In March of that year, 1980, our first baby, little Joanne, was born. The pregnancy had not been planned but Sue was very happy that she was expecting a baby. I was over the moon. I came from a large family and I loved babies.

The birth wasn't easy. Those were hard days in the hospital. Sue was only 19 years old and having her first baby. I was only 17.

She was in labour for thirty-six hours, at which stage the doctor told her she was to have an emergency caesarean. She was in agony, exhausted from the long labour and terrified at the prospect of having an operation.

Although Joanne was a very beautiful brown-eyed, dark-haired baby, the doctors had some difficult news. When they came to tell us, Joanne was in Sue's arms.

'Joanne's feet are twisted upwards.'

'What does that mean?' we asked.

'It means that at some time in the future she will need a plaster of Paris and then physiotherapy to bring them back into position.'

Then came some more bad news.

'Joanne also has a cleft on her soft palate and isn't able to drink properly.'

From then on, Joanne was given a bottle with a lamb's teat (where the hole is on one side) so that the milk could be directed down her throat when she fed.

The hospital staff were fantastic and when Joanne was nine months old, she went back to have her cleft palate corrected. We also had to keep going back to have her feet newly plastered on a monthly basis from the age of four months up until she was a year old. When she was one year old, they made special boots for her to wear which supported her ankles. We just got on with it and did the best we could for her. She was such a darling and we loved her very much. It didn't matter to us that she had these differences, our only concern was that she wasn't in pain and that she would be OK.

Sue was in a difficult position. Ever since I had taken her away from her parents to the squat, apart from the short truce a long time before, her mum and dad wouldn't have anything to do with me. This cut her off from her family and as time went on and Joanne came along, Sue really wanted to see her parents. She wanted them to meet their little granddaughter. She missed them and her three brothers, whom she hadn't seen for a whole year. I encouraged her to start going back on short visits.

On one of those visits, seeing that Sue had no intention of leaving me and realizing that I was the father of their grandchild, Sue's mum and dad asked to see me again. That first meeting was difficult but the door of healing had opened a little and over the coming months, it widened. I was finally accepted into the family and I developed a strong friendship with Sue's brothers.

Sue was so happy. She had her family back.

Not long after Joanne was born, we moved out of my brother's place, this time into my mum and dad's home. We longed for our own place and my parents helped by lending us enough to buy our own caravan. It was our first proper home and we loved it. It was heaven; apart from when Joanne was crying or keeping us both awake half the night! We didn't care, we adored her. But moving into our own place and having little Joanne still didn't change my lifestyle. I continued to fight, take drugs and drink heavily. Nothing changed. In fact, it was getting worse.

At one point I decided to try a harder drug. It was my first and only experience of LSD. I was in the pub one night and I bought two tablets from a mate. Like everything else I did at that time, I overdid it. I should have only taken half a tablet for the first time, but instead I took both of them at once, downing them with several beers. Sue was at my mum and dad's place with little Joanne while I was down the pub dropping acid.

After three quarters of an hour, I started hallucinating and I tried to get back home. I don't remember much about it but I've been told that I stood in a phone box for two hours, just staring out through the glass. I don't remember that. A friend found me there and all I could say to him was, 'Leave me alone.' In the end, he gave me a lift home. It was a horrible experience. I walked up the level driveway to my mum and dad's place and it felt like I was walking up a really steep hill. I was seeing lots of monsters coming out of the doorposts. I was terrified. My eyes were dilated and my mouth was distorted with terror.

When Sue saw the state I was in, she shouted at me. She was so scared. I didn't tell her I had taken LSD, I just said someone had spiked my drink. I told her to let me lie down and I would be OK.

That was a bad trip. The next thing I remember I was sitting on my mum and dad's bed. My mum was scared. I was in a bad way.

When I opened my eyes, I looked up at them both and groaned, 'I don't know how I got here.'

My mum grabbed my dad's arm. 'Joe, he's finally gone,' she said, crying as she held onto him.

They had to call the doctor for me. When everyone had left me alone with the doctor I told him what I'd taken. He was fantastic. He took my hand and reassured me it would be OK and told me to sleep it off. It took all night before I came out of it. It felt like a nightmare that didn't go away even when I woke up. It was a terrifying experience which I never forgot. It put me off LSD for life but it didn't put me off anything else. In fact, Joanne made her first visit to court when she was just two weeks old. She lay in her mother's arms as she waited to see what the sentence would be for her father this time.

I had been involved in another big fight at the chip shop, this time with a couple of lads, one who had bitten my thumb hard and made it bleed. The fight was so bad that my two mates and my younger brother were arrested on the spot and taken to a cell. I managed to get away but I felt guilty. It was unfair that I was free and they weren't, so I said to Sue, 'I have to go to the police station to sort this out.'

'No, leave it Larry,' she begged, 'Just lie low.'

But I couldn't allow my little brother and my friends to be locked up without a protest, so I left the house and headed for the police station. When I arrived, I walked up to the counter, ready to give the policeman a piece of my mind but it didn't turn out quite the way I had hoped. The desk sergeant took one look at me and leaned over the counter.

'Are you Larry Harvey?'

'Yes.'

'Then you're under arrest.'

He grabbed me by the arm and promptly locked me in a cell, where I spent the night.

Not long after that, I stood in court, with my girlfriend and newborn baby waiting outside the courtroom. The judge sentenced me to 180 hours of community service. I got off lightly for that one, due to the fact that Joanne was only two weeks old.

My community service took place helping in a centre for people with learning difficulties. After working all day in my father's scrapyard, I had to gobble my tea and rush over to the centre to play cards and dance with the folk. I really enjoyed my time there and they appreciated the effort I was making. Then later on, I visited a youth club once a week to help with the kids. I knew this youth club well already; I'd broken into it when I was 12 years old. When I was there to help, I actually enjoyed it because I wasn't drugged up or drunk. I liked the people and got on well with them. Working with young people brought out a softer side of me.

Not long after starting my community service, I started going out with my brothers and nephew to a club called "The Millionaires' Club". They held grudge match boxing there. One night, during a fight, the boxer hit the floor hard and his head was really hurt, so the fight had to be stopped. I was dying to get in the ring and as I knew the referee Martin had done some boxing, I called out to him,

"Alright Martin, why don't you clear the ring and you and I can have a fight?"

He agreed and I climbed into the ring. It was a good fight, but a long one. In the end, after a right royal battle, the referee put both our hands in the air - it was a draw!

So, life was still as hectic as ever. I was taking drugs, drinking and fighting. Meanwhile, I had a new baby, a new home, and I was trying to hold down a job. And now I had to do community service too.

Would it all catch up with me one day?

I never stopped to ask.

Chapter 7

BANGED UP

The drug-taking didn't prevent me from doing the difficult, physical work I had learned from my father. I was a hard worker and that didn't change. As well as the scrap metal business, I branched out on my own and started a couple of new ventures. I sold horse manure in bags, door to door. Then I got into demolition and waste disposal. I moved about two hundred tons of rubbish a week, including asbestos; we weren't aware it was dangerous in those days. Mainly though, I was dealing drugs and receiving stolen goods. As the months went by, this became my life.

The fighting continued. In fact, one particularly nasty fight led to a really bad battle on my own land. Over twenty police officers arrived and things became so bad that they brought in police dogs too. I was in the thick of the fighting when I heard a cry. I turned to see one of my nephews being tackled to the ground by the police Alsatian. I was frightened by what I saw, so I grabbed a nearby broom and charged up to the dog to try to get it off the boy. The handler saw me approaching. I was wild-eyed and had a stick in my hand, so he let the dog go. The dog didn't waste a second; it raced up to me and bit me hard on the arm. I was arrested and taken to hospital where I had twenty-one stitches in my arm. The next day I had to attend a special court, because it was during the Christmas period, and then it was off to Horfield Prison to be held on remand.

The inevitable had finally happened.

I was in prison and this time it was an adult prison. The court decided I was not to be allowed out in the community this time and alongside my brother, I was remanded in custody for three months.

It was a whole new experience and not a good one.

My brother and I were held together in Horfield Prison, Bristol, on one of the wings on the fourth landing. Even though I had my brother with me, it was still a big shock. We were locked in a tiny cell for up to twenty-three hours a day, every day, with no toilet, just a bucket between us. Every morning we were made to 'slop out' along with the rest of the prisoners. I hated the shouts of the men and guards. I hated the clang of the metal doors. I hated the smell and the humiliation of taking that bucket out each morning to empty into the toilet in front of the prison officers. I hated it all.

Every day, we would sit in our cells for hours and hours listening to the radio, eating, smoking, and trying to sleep. There was no television and nothing else to do. One hour in each day we were allowed to go outside to walk in the grey concrete yard, round and round in small circles. For another hour each day we could receive visitors. Once a week we had social time or 'sosh' as the men called it, when we could meet other prisoners, play table tennis and watch television for one hour only.

Once, our dad tried to get us out on bail but it was refused. Sue was as loyal as ever and came six days a week to visit me. I behaved myself in prison and managed to stay out of trouble. Without the alcohol and drugs, I was a great bloke, friendly and popular and funny. With alcohol and drugs, I was a very different person and I was always ready for a fight. I just found it all too difficult to give up, they had such a strong hold on me.

Being in Horfield Prison was a depressing experience and I felt very down, especially as I knew the charge of hitting the policeman was a false one. I felt very strongly that I didn't deserve to be there. On the few occasions when I was on my own, I shed tears of despair and wondered when it would all end. It was the injustice of it all and the separation from Sue, the baby and the rest of the world, that got me down most of all. I felt alienated from the rest of society, just as I had done at school. I couldn't see any light at the end of the tunnel because I didn't know when I was going to get out of prison. I became very bitter towards the police and saw my solicitor as often as I could. I wanted to get out of prison and back home as soon as possible.

Amongst it all though, there were a few brighter moments. Some of the prison officers were kind and I received no prejudice for being a Gypsy from either them or the other inmates, which surprised me.

Every Sunday morning, there was a Christian service we could go to in the prison chapel. Through all my troubles, I had always believed that there was a God somewhere. I just hadn't done anything about it, but in prison I started attending the service every Sunday.

I sat, staring intently ahead at the painting on the wall above the altar, listening to the sermon. I never understood a word of what the chaplain was talking about. It didn't mean anything to me. I was more struck by the fact that the congregation had divided themselves into a black side and a white side. Racial discrimination was the norm. I decided to break that norm by sitting defiantly on the black side, mainly because I had good friends at the Empire Boxing Club who were black. The black prisoners had similar backgrounds to me. Some of them were used to being on the outside of society too. That action of mine led eventually to everyone mixing together in the chapel. There were no more black and white sides in that place of peace.

I even put my name down for the weekly Bible study, but for some reason I was never called to attend. There were many reasons why this may have happened; my name could have been left off the list one week and never put back on it, or there might not have been enough officers on duty that day to escort me out of my cell. I never did find out the reasons, but it added to my gloom. As day after day passed, I began to despair and wonder if I would ever get out. I was in a deep depression and cried many tears alone in my cell. As the months passed, I felt worse and worse, until one exciting day I was called to court so that I could request bail. To my horror, it was refused. I was taken back into the van and driven back to my cell. That was a really dark day. The hope of getting out made still being there much worse.

Locked up in my cell once again, in desperation I decided I would pray to God every night before I went to bed. Not just formal prayers but a real conversation.

'God, get me out of here, I'm sorry for what I've done. I just can't stand it in here.'

One night whilst I was praying, I felt God answer me with a very clear sentence. I heard it in my head.

'Larry, you're going to get out tomorrow.'

It was such a strong impression that I was certain God had spoken to me. I knew it was going to happen.

I sat up in bed, full of excitement and shook my brother awake in the next bunk.

'Pete! God has told me we'll be out tomorrow!'

'Bob? Bob who?'

'Not Bob, Pete! God!'

'Go to sleep Larry.'

And with that, he turned over, pulled the blanket up over his head and went back to sleep himself. But I couldn't sleep. I was too excited. I just knew something was going to happen.

The next day our solicitor once again applied for bail. We waited for a call from him, telling us that we were going to be released immediately. But the phone call didn't come. Time went on and still no call. I began to lose hope. Had I imagined that voice? It got later and later until it was visiting hour. As we were being searched before the visit I told the officer, 'Can you be careful when searching my left arm please, because it's still painful from the bite from the police dog?'

'I hope the dog's OK, Harvey,' he said, laughing.

'Harvey, is it?' piped in one of the other officers. 'I heard that name earlier on in reception.'

I was excited. Hearing you name in reception meant you might be on the list for bail. 'We're expecting to hear from our solicitors regarding bail.' I told him.

'Well don't build your hopes up. I may have got it wrong,' he replied. I felt deflated, again.

When Sue arrived, she could see that I was upset. I was angry too and my anger turned to panic. Maybe I hadn't really heard from God. Maybe I'd imagined it all? The visiting hour continued and still there was no phone call to tell me I had been released. Sitting in the visitor's hall with Sue I could feel myself getting angrier and I was starting to kick up a fuss. It was not a good sign; things could turn ugly.

At that moment, the phone rang. An officer answered it, listened for a few moments and turned to me and Pete. A smile broke out on his face as he spoke down the phone. And I heard him say,

'No, we're going to keep the Harveys here forever.'

I stood up, that was terrible news. I was ready for a fight now. The officer put the phone down and grinned.

'You're free,' he said.

I was ecstatic.

I had heard from God after all! It was true!

I went back to my cell, collected my things and walked out through the metal gates and back into the world. Sue met me at the front door and we hugged. I was on a curfew and had to be home and inside every night by seven in the evening, but I didn't care because I was free.

When the charge eventually came up in court twelve months later, it was dropped from affray (a very violent offence) to disturbing the peace. The serious charge of attempting to assault a police officer was also dropped. Somewhere along the line the broom I had picked up had changed to an iron bar. The evidence against me was that I had tried to hit the police officer, who had ducked, and I attempted to hit him again with the iron bar. I learned years later that the iron bar evidence was given to cover the over enthusiastic action by the dog, which had caused my twenty-one stitches.

Even though my time in prison was horrible and even though I knew my encounter with God was real, nothing seemed to be able to steer me away from the lifestyle in which I was caught. I went straight back onto cannabis, having my first smoke in months the first night I was out.

But other things began to change. As I grew older and time went on, I discovered new, more sophisticated ways of getting an income. Through friends, I began to receive stolen caravans to order and learned how to rub out the identity number and replace it with a false one; I was so good at this that I was never caught. There was a huge market for second-hand caravans at the time and we made a lot of money. I also started to sell stolen MOTs and bought a big book of false insurance cover notes for twenty pounds, selling them for twenty pounds each. I sold false tax discs too and at one point I even dealt in counterfeit money. I passed on stolen credit cards, sold stolen mountain bikes, ride-on lawnmowers, new televisions, transit vans and lorries and I advertised them all openly in the papers. I was making a lot of money.

All the time I was dealing in stolen goods I was running my own successful, legitimate business as well. I owned a fleet of lorries and had several men working for me in a small demolition and waste disposal company that I started up. Sue kept the books meticulously. And something else had changed too. The one thing I didn't deal in now was drugs. I had turned against it, after I realized how much harm they caused. Whilst it was OK for me to still smoke cannabis, I didn't want anyone else to be hurt by passing on drugs to other people. Besides, I could make good money in other ways.

One day, I was out in my lorry when I was horrified to witness an old lady getting knocked over by a car. I jumped out of the lorry with my brother Pete and my nephew Henry. While they were putting their coats under her head, I went to find help. I asked the landlord in a nearby pub to call an ambulance. I was so upset by the whole thing that he thought it had been my own mother who had been involved in the accident. The ambulance arrived and took the poor old lady to hospital. When I arrived home that evening, I was in floods of tears and I told Sue what had happened. I tried to visit the old lady in hospital and to take her some chocolates, but I was never allowed to know who she was. I still think about her and hope she recovered.

On the outside, life was good. If we wanted anything, we could buy it new with the money we were making.

Our family was growing too.

We had a second child. Little Larry Junior. He was born in April

1984. He was an exact miniature of me and we adored him. He had a shock of black hair and dark brown eyes and he crawled around happily after his big sister Joanne, who by now was 4 years old. Six years later, Joanne and Larry Junior were joined by a baby sister, Samantha. Sam was born in 1990. I loved being a father.

When Larry Junior was 8 years old, he would sometimes come to work with me in the lorry. One day as I was talking to a customer, little Larry asked me if he could push the wheelbarrow, full of bricks, up the high planks on to the lorry.

'No,' I said. 'You'll not be able to do it.'

The next thing I noticed was little Larry running past me pushing the wheelbarrow. He raced up the planks and onto the lorry! So when I next went to train at the Empire Sports Club I told the owner what little Larry had done with the wheelbarrow.

'Bring him down one Sunday morning,' he said. 'We'll see what he can do.'

Larry eventually became a four-time British Weight Lifting Champion and was in the under 16's England team. We were so proud of him.

To anyone looking in from the outside, our family was a picture of domestic bliss. We appeared normal and happy but all the wheeling and dealing and contacts with the underworld continued in secret. This brought in the money and paid for our very comfortable lifestyle but underneath it all, we were worried and highly stressed. Worried about getting caught by the police. And stressed the whole time with the strain of it all. It wasn't the comfortable life it appeared to be. But that didn't mean I was going to give it all up. I just decided I would have to be more careful. But could our lifestyle really continue for much longer?

Chapter 8

DRUNK AND DISORDERLY

Even with all the things money could buy, Sue and I were not happy. We argued all the time. Sue began to hate what alcohol and drugs were doing to me. She wanted me to stop or at least cut down.

When we were younger, she didn't mind me going out to the pub every night, but as we got older and the children were growing up, we began to argue about the fact that I was going out all the time, getting drunk and smoking dope. Sue finally reached the stage where she began to realise this was not the life she wanted. The day after I'd been drinking I would be in a foul mood and this caused more and more arguments.

'Can't you stay in just some evenings of the week and not leave me all alone?' she begged. 'Couldn't you come home sober, just once and have a sensible conversation with me?'

The answer was 'no, I couldn't,' because the alcohol and the drugs were much too attractive. They had a bigger hold on me than my family.

I just couldn't see it at the time.

Things got so bad that finally, Sue had had enough. We'd been arguing a lot and I had gone out drinking again. Sue brought the children to the pub and asked me to go outside.

'I want you to come home,' she said.

'No,' I growled. 'I don't want to. And if you don't like it, you can clear off.'

I was drunk. With that, Sue took the children home, grabbed some clothes and called a taxi to take her and the kids to a local hostel for women. Her plan was to be added to the council tenancy waiting list so she could be rehoused with the children. In the end, she only stayed there a week because the police telephoned her and informed her that I had gone to the police station and begged them to lock me up. I couldn't stand being without them. The police asked Sue to call me as they were worried I might harm myself. She telephoned me and I went to meet her. I was in a terrible state. We talked for a long time and I eventually persuaded her to come home.

'On one condition,' she said.

'What?'

'You only go out twice a week, not every night.'

'I promise,' I said. 'And I promise I'll change.'

Sue went back to the hostel, packed her things, collected the children and came home with me. It was the wakeup call I badly needed.

But it didn't solve everything in our relationship by a long way.

A lot of things still needed to be talked through. Because of this, I suggested we go away with the kids for a few days. It was a good move. During those days, we decided to try and make another go of it and I promised again that I would cut down on the drink and drugs.

But the promise didn't last long. I went out to the pub one night soon after with my brother Pete and on the way home spotted a police van packed with officers. Still longing for the thrill, I purposely dropped my chip papers in front of them. I wanted them to chase me, and they did, but when they pulled up and I started to run, I fell over. Straightaway, four police officers jumped on me, dragged me into the police van and started to hit me in the face. The next day, I had two black eyes and I couldn't see properly. I went to court and was fined £100 for being drunk and disorderly.

Things were returning to 'normal' but Sue thought constantly about the reality of what we were doing. The money, the drugs and the alcohol didn't mask the worry of being found out, or the possibility that the police could turn up at any moment and arrest us. It meant I would go back to prison and it wouldn't just be me this time. Sue was involved now. Our children could be taken away from us and that was unthinkable. The children meant the world to us. It was not a happy time. Although we had everything we could possibly want in terms of material things; a new washing machine, fridge, fancy cars, holidays, designer clothes, none of it brought lasting happiness for us.

Our kids were amazing though, growing up strong and happy, unaware of the tensions around them. There was even a surprise addition in 1997, when Sue was told she was expecting twins. Our two little girls, Billie-Jo and Georgie Lee, were born on the 2nd April 1997 at St Michael's Hospital, Bristol. Sue and I were thrilled to bits.

The promise I made to Sue not to drink too much alcohol was broken again shortly after that. As I set off to Wellington in Somerset to a family christening one day, Sue begged me not to drink, but I found the temptation impossible to resist. All of my family and acquaintances were there and they were all drinking. I wasn't going to be left out.

Eventually, the inevitable happened and some of the guests turned ugly. Outside the pub, a fight broke out. This time I was the one who suffered when someone bit into the top of my ear. I fell down a few times and hit the kerb and I was so drunk I couldn't even see the other person. By this time, the police had been called. A young policewoman arrived at the scene and in her panic, sprayed my face with CS gas- tear gas - and incredibly painful. I was taken, eyes streaming and gasping for breath, to hospital to have stitches where I'd hit the kerb. We had all sworn to have another fight when I was sober, but that didn't happen.

Something far worse was about to happen instead.

Things calmed down a bit and our babies continued to grow. They were gorgeous but they were also a handful. Coping with one new baby was difficult enough, coping with two newborns together was something else.

Being part of a Gypsy family though, meant we were always

supported, always had the family nearby, and could always turn to someone for help. Sue soon learned that was true. In the early years she was never really left alone, as we lived next door to my mum and dad, and my sister and her children lived there too. However, in the later years when my sister and her children moved away to Devon, Sue felt a bit more isolated, even though Joanne was 16 when the twins were born and was a wonderful help with them. I was also doing my bit by that time and I was at home much more and not going out every night. I adored the kids and I tried really hard to be a hands-on dad, taking my turn to feed one of the twins during the night, while Sue fed the other. Sue tells me that I often left for work the next morning with my eyeballs out on my cheeks from tiredness.

Life went on and was as hectic as usual, until, in 1998, when the twins were just one year old, something happened which would completely change our lives.

Joanne had had ongoing health problems since she was born, but she was as happy and as strong as she could be and coped cheerfully with whatever came her way. Now, aged just 18, she developed a secondary infection in her elbow from an operation she had had on her lower back. It wouldn't heal and it was getting worse and worse. She had to have it continually drained and bandaged. By January 1999, it was so bad that she was sent to see a plastic surgeon.

Sue travelled with her to nearby Frenchay Hospital in Bristol, a world-famous centre for neurosurgery. There they met the consultant.

'We'll need to operate,' he said, examining Joanne's elbow. 'But it's not urgent. I might be able to do it at the end of this month.'

Sue, Joanne and I weren't too worried. It was just one of quite a few operations that Joanne had been having and would continue to have.

This time, however, it would be very different.

Chapter 9

'SAVE OUR JOANNE!'

After they had been to see the consultant, Sue and Joanne decided to have a coffee in the hospital café before driving home. They were sitting chatting about what they were going to do that evening, when Sue became aware of a man standing by their table. She looked up. She had never seen him before and was wondering why he was there.

'Can I help you?' Sue asked.

He looked down at them both.

'Is this your daughter?'

'Yes, this is Joanne.'

The man looked a bit uncomfortable. He had a strange look on his face.

'I feel that God has told me I need to pray for you both. Can I ask why you are here today?'

Sue was immediately suspicious. Why would a complete stranger want to pray for them? What was he up to? But rather than make a fuss in front of everybody, she told him about Joanne's upcoming minor operation and agreed to let him say a short prayer for them. When he'd finished, the man smiled and turned to walk away.

'God bless,' he said and went back to his table.

What was all that about?

Out of all the people in the café, why had he chosen them?

Sue was mystified.

When she arrived home, she told me all about their experience and I agreed it was very strange. A couple of hours after that we forgot all about it, as the phone rang. It was the hospital to say there had been a cancellation and Joanne's operation had been brought forward to the next morning.

After we had got used to the idea, we rushed around and tried to pack Joanne's overnight bag, as well as making arrangements for someone to look after the children. The plan was that Sue would take Joanne to hospital and I would come in later with the twins.

The next morning, Joanne settled quickly in her hospital room and was given her pre-medication by the doctor. Sue had mentioned to the nurse that for the last few days, Joanne had been falling asleep a lot during the day.

'She's probably nervous about the operation,' the nurse said.

Sue leaned over Joanne and chatted to her in order keep her mind off everything going on around her.

This was the moment when our lives changed forever.

Joanne stopped breathing.

Her eyes were staring ahead, fixed.

She wasn't moving.

Sue screamed, 'Nurse! Nurse, she's not breathing!'

'Don't be silly Mrs Harvey.'

'She is *not* breathing!' Sue screamed even louder.

The nurse still didn't believe her, but then she leaned over Joanne and saw for herself. She hit the emergency button.

Bells rang, nurses and doctors rushed into the room, along with the resuscitation trolley.

The crash team sprang into action.

Meanwhile, I was back at home getting the twins ready, unaware of the horrible drama taking place just a few miles away. The phone rang. It was Sue, frantic and in tears.

'Larry! She's stopped breathing.'

I couldn't believe what I was hearing. I ran out of our caravan over to my parents' home opposite.

'Help, help!' I cried.

My parents rushed out straightaway and as soon as they heard what had happened, they offered to take care of the twins so I could go to the hospital.

My brother George, his wife Pauline and I jumped into the car and George sped away from the house. I prayed and cried the whole way there.

'Please God, don't let her be dead. Don't let her be dead.'

The car skidded to a stop outside the hospital entrance. I got out and ran up the stairs to Joanne's room.

A doctor stopped me on my way. 'Are you Mr. Harvey?'

'Don't tell me she's dead, please.'

'No, she's alright, but we don't know why it's happened. She's in intensive care.'

The next few days were a blur for us. Our families arrived within the hour to support us and they never left us throughout the crisis. No Gypsy family would dream of doing anything else.

Over the next few days, the word spread throughout our community and at one point over a hundred members of the family, aunts, uncles, nieces, nephews and cousins had all gathered together in the hospital.

The staff said they had never seen anything like it.

All the comfort and support in the world couldn't change the situation. That first night when Joanne was in the Intensive Treatment Unit the doctors came to speak to Sue and me.

'Joanne will need to have scans and tests in the morning.'

'What's wrong with her?'

'We don't know.'

The hours dragged by and the wait was agonizing.

I turned to Sue.

'I need to talk to the doctor,' I whispered.

The staff got one of the on-call doctors on the phone for me.

I drew a deep breath. 'You're looking for a tumour, aren't you?' I asked.

'Yes, we are,' the doctor replied.

I put the phone down, distraught. I left the hospital, got into my car and drove, sobbing, through the pouring wind and rain. I somehow arrived at my Aunt Margie's caravan, a few miles down the road. I banged on the door, still in tears. My aunt was ready with her answer when I told her I didn't know what to do.

'Larry, you've got to have faith. Where's your faith?'

I drove back to the hospital but I couldn't find my faith.

When the scan results came back, they showed a massive cyst on Joanne's brainstem, caused by the top of her spine, her odontoid peg, growing abnormally into her brainstem. It was explained to us that the brainstem controls our breathing and many other of our vital life signs and the pressure the cyst was causing on her brainstem was seriously endangering her life.

We were told that we would need to see the neurosurgeon, Mr Bolger, but we would have to wait until 5 o'clock on Thursday for his opinion.

Sue and I were on a false high; Joanne had made it through the last few days, so she would be alright, wouldn't she?

The surgeon arrived on the dot at 5 p.m., accompanied by a nurse. He looked very smart in his suit and tie. They both looked grave and asked Sue and I to sit down. I leaned forward.

'She's going to be alright, isn't she?'

'I don't know.'

After that we barely heard anything the surgeon said, until the words, 'Only one in the world to be performed, if you agree to it.' We had to ask him to repeat it all.

'I can operate on Joanne, but this particular operation has never been performed before and the odds of her living through it are extremely low.'

We sat still, shocked and in silence.

'We will need to do it by what we call "stealth" surgery, a technique I learnt in America. That is, using instruments developed for the space programme in the States. We will have to get the instruments from another part of the UK, as we don't have them here in Bristol.

It is a very delicate operation. We will need to go in through the mouth to get to this particular bone.'

I couldn't stand to hear any more. 'I've got to go,' I said and I left the room.

My sister Kathy and the rest of the family were waiting in the hospital lounge outside when I walked in. When they saw how devastated I was, they became very upset too, so much so that the surgeon, who came out after me, said to them, 'You've got to pull yourselves together. Your brother needs you.' He was right. For the next agonising eight days, Sue and I could barely eat or sleep. We never left Joanne alone, day or night and most of the family slept at the hospital. We made sure at least one of us was always with her.

Our worry worsened when a week later we were told that a famous visiting neurosurgeon had told Joanne's surgeon, 'I would recommend you leave her. I wouldn't touch her. It's too risky.'

We clutched at anything that might help Joanne. I remembered some conversations I had with a 'Minister to Travellers' who used to be a friend to the Gypsies around Bristol, a man called Cliff Kelly. Cliff was always asking me to go with him to a big church in the centre of Bristol called Pip' n 'Jay. I had never gone with him and I had never intended to go either, but today I was desperate.

'I'm going down to that Pip' n' Jay church,' I said to Sue. 'I'm going to touch the walls of the church and pray.'

Over the next few days, my brothers, my nephew and I drove down almost every night, sometimes at two and three in the morning, through the empty city streets and parked in the dark churchyard. I would walk up to the walls of the church, put my hands on them and call out to God, if there was a God, to help us.

As well as the family, the hospital chaplain, Colin, tried to help us during this terrible time. We had got to know Colin well over the few days Joanne had been in the ITU. He had talked with us and tried to comfort us as much as he could but for me, people in dog collars meant only death. I had seen too many of them and only at funerals.

Colin passed me in the ITU one day and on this occasion, I grabbed him. 'Please tell God that I want to change places with our Joanne. Please make Him do it.'

'Larry, you know you can't do that,' he said gently. He refused to give me false hope, but he prayed with me for Joanne and he asked God to be with us.

The day of the operation arrived and I was in such a state of anxiety that I could hardly cope with it. I had barely slept for the last few weeks and in the early hours of the morning, I headed down to A & E to ask for help to be able to sleep. They knew who I was; the whole hospital was aware of our situation because Joanne's operation had never been performed before. It was to be the first of its kind in the world.

'Please can someone give me something to knock me out?' I begged them. 'I can't cope.'

One of the A & E doctors came over and put his arm round me. He pressed two tablets into my hand.

'Here, they'll put you out during the operation Larry. Go home and get some rest.'

I put the tablets in my hand and walked outside the hospital doors into the cold wind and rain, but suddenly I couldn't go home. I couldn't take the tablets either. I knew I needed to be there and I knew I needed to be awake. I had to face it. I turned around and walked back into the hospital.

I was still unable to sleep at 6 a.m., so decided to walk to the hospital chapel. I could barely contain my worry and grief as I opened the heavy doors and walked into the little room. It was empty, cold and silent. I walked down its narrow aisle to the altar at the end. I never cried as much in all my life as I did then. I fell to my knees in agony in front of the cross on the altar.

'Lord, if you're there and you exist, save our Joanne. I can't live if she doesn't.'

My prayer was met with total silence.

Then something amazing happened. The despair and the grief that had been eating me up inside for so long was completely taken away in one moment. In its place was a wave of total peace. There was a warmth which washed through me from the top of my head to the soles of my feet. It was an overwhelming sense of complete calm and as I knelt there, I knew, without a doubt, that Joanne would live. I had never been so sure of anything in my life.

I took a moment to drink in this amazing feeling, then I leapt to my feet, bursting with strength. I ran along the hospital corridors and back into the ITU, like a new person. Sue was sleeping across Joanne's bed and I shook her gently to waken her.

'Sue, she's going to be alright! She's going to be alright!'

'What do you mean?'

'I went into the chapel and I had this amazing experience with God. Our Joanne is going to be alright.'

Sue's reaction wasn't what I expected. She thought I had finally lost my mind. In fact, I later learned that the family had been so worried about me over those few days that my father asked my brothers and nephews to keep a special eye on me. And now, one minute I was distraught and hardly able to bear the situation and then suddenly, I was exclaiming to everyone that my daughter was going to be alright! I couldn't convince anyone that what had happened to me in the chapel was true, no matter what I said. But I knew with absolute certainty that it was.

The first operation was due to start at 9 a.m. that morning and I was still in a state of peace from what had happened.

'Come on, we'll go to Pip' n' Jay and see if someone can pray for us,' I said to Sue.

Larry Junior and I helped Sue to her feet. She could barely stand under the weight of exhaustion and worry. In the car on the way to the church, she started to sob.

'Larry, you keep saying she's going to be alright, but how do you know?'

I just kept driving. I didn't answer her straightaway but suddenly a strange thought came into my head.

'Look,' I said, 'I'll prove it to you. The person who's going to meet us will be called John. I just know that's what his name will be.' I don't know why I said it, or where the thought came from, but I just felt I had to say it.

We arrived at the big old church and parked in the churchyard. We went around the side, where there was a light on. I banged on the side door, which was locked. We heard footsteps inside and the turn of a key. A man opened it. We explained to him how we used to know Cliff Kelly, who used to go to Pip' n' Jay. The man opened the door wider.

'Come in,' he said. 'You're welcome. My name's John.'

He led us in, sat down with us and prayed with us for Joanne.

Some weeks later, we were to learn just how strange it was that John had opened the door that morning. Someone else, a lady, had gone to answer the door when suddenly she was overcome with a strange feeling and had to sit down to recover. John had said to her, 'Don't worry, I'll go.'

After the prayer with John, we left the church and drove back to the hospital and headed straight to the chapel. Sue wanted to see the place where I had had such a strange experience. When she heard my story again and saw how sure I was, she began slowly to be convinced that I was right. God had heard me. Somehow, in spite of all the odds, Joanne was going to be OK. Still, we were human and we were terrified of seeing the surgeon. Joanne was prepped and taken down to theatre. We must have paced that quarter-mile long, dreary corridor seventy or eighty times during the next few hours as Joanne was having her operation. All of our family were with us.

At midnight, fifteen hours after the operation had begun, my sister spotted a man in an operating gown walking towards us.

'Is that Mr Bolger?' she asked.

My feet were stuck to the floor. I couldn't move.

Eventually the surgeon reached us and took off his mask. His expression didn't appear too promising. We feared the worst but the news was better than we could have hoped.

'We think it's been a success.'

Mr Bolger smiled and shook our hands and there was much cheering and clapping from the whole family.

Our prayers had truly been answered. She was alive.

Chapter 10

WELCOME HOME

Joanne was out of danger but she was still very poorly. Sue and I were at last allowed in to see her after she was wheeled back from theatre. We couldn't wait to reach her bed in the corner of the Intensive Care Unit. We had been warned that she would be hooked up to all sorts of machines and be very swollen, but it was still a terrible shock to see the countless tubes she had reaching out from her face and body. Multiple beeps were coming from every machine and Joanne lay amongst them looking so small and vulnerable. We leaned over to touch her. We had tried to be prepared, but nothing could prepare us for how she looked that day. Her face was blown up like a football. We hardly recognized our own daughter. We sat by her bed, praying and willing her to get better.

There was one more operation to come. On the Wednesday of the same week, at 2 p.m., we once again went through the ordeal of watching Joanne wheeled down the corridor into the operating theatre. We were told the operation would take five hours. It took fifteen. We spent that long day and night pacing backwards and forwards between the chapel and the canteen, praying, drinking countless cups of coffee and reminding ourselves of the amazing peace I had felt before the first operation and the assurance I had been given that she would survive.

The wait was agonizing and it seemed like it would never end. At one point we stopped an intensive care nurse coming out of the theatre.

'Are there any problems?' we asked.

'They've just rung down to say they have to take bone grafts from her hip,' she replied, but assured us everything else was going well.

Midnight came and went. 1 o'clock in the morning. 2 o'clock. At 4 a.m., Mr. Bolger at last came into the waiting room.

'She's still alive, but the next forty-eight hours are touch and go, because she's had such a lot done. You can see her in a couple of hours, when we've got her back to ICU.'

We were so relieved but still under terrible strain. We went back to the room the hospital had given us, exhausted. Collapsing onto the bed we fell asleep, though we didn't mean to.

After what seemed like only five minutes, we were woken by a loud, insistent bell. We sat up to see the red light flashing on the telephone which ran direct to the ICU. My heart raced and leapt into my mouth. *This is it,* I thought. *Terrible news.* I plucked up all the courage I could muster and lifted the receiver.

'What? Oh, yes. Thanks.'

What a relief. It turned out we had asked to be woken early so that we could go and see Joanne as soon as she was ready, but we had completely forgotten we had asked!

Now wide awake, we went down to the ICU to see her. There she lay, face blown up again, so much so that we couldn't see her eyes or mouth. We knew she was still in danger for the next forty-eight hours, but we were just so relieved and thankful to see her alive.

Things progressed and after several weeks in the ICU, Joanne was well enough to be moved to the High Dependency Unit. Sue and I stayed by her side almost constantly. My nieces looked after the twins and took turns cooking and keeping the house going for the other children. All in all, Joanne was in hospital recovering for four months. During that time I found it really difficult to face my other children. All they wanted to know was whether Joanne was going to be OK and I couldn't answer that with all honesty. She was still very poorly.

Amidst all the sitting around and waiting for things to get better, I decided to go out one day and buy Joanne a Walkman portable cassette player. She loved music and it would be a great way for her to listen to all her own choices. I went into the shop, looked at all the ones on offer and bought the best one I could find. When the salesman asked me to sign the two-year guarantee, I signed it, picked up the bag and left the shop to go back to the hospital. But once outside, a thought came into my head. I stopped, turned around and went back into the shop. The salesman looked up in surprise. I put the Walkman down on the counter.

'You've got the guarantee in my name, but I need it to be in my daughter's name. I want her to be able to come back in two years if there's something wrong with it. She's going to be able to walk into this shop like I'm doing now. Please change it for me.'

The salesman took the guarantee, ripped it up and gave me a new one for Joanne to sign herself. I was praying and I was determined that Joanne was going to be well enough take back her own Walkman if necessary. That was how sure I was that she was going to get better.

Joanne couldn't move for many weeks and as she lay in bed hooked up to multiple machines, she had visits from loads of members of our family and friends. They kept her going through that difficult time, but not everybody was allowed in to see her. Joanne was so ill that the hospital kept a close watch on who could come in and who couldn't. She had so many relatives that she would have been overwhelmed if everyone who wanted to see her was allowed to come.

One person in particular who came in to see her was my sister Kathy, who visited on a regular basis. One of Joanne's cousins would also come in to rub her feet with cream, paint her toenails, wet wipe her face and give her a lovely manicure. Joanne loved it. Her other cousins would arrive, bringing her favourite meals which they had cooked especially for her. In particular, a good friend of the family, Rob, knew that Joanne was a fan of Naseem Hamed, the world champion boxer, and just for Joanne he managed to get hold of a signed photo of him. That photo held pride of place on Joanne's bedside cabinet on the ward. She was a lucky girl to have such a loving family and good friends around her. The doctors were sure that all the support she was receiving was helping to make her strong again.

Towards the end of Joanne's stay Sue and I were sitting in the hospital canteen one day having a well-earned break, when Sue looked across the room, did a double take and grabbed my arm.

'That's the man who asked if he could pray for us when Joanne and I first came here.' she said.

I got up and walked over to him. We introduced ourselves and I told 'Smiley Steve', as we called him when we got to know him better, the whole story of Joanne's near brush with death, her resuscitation, the dangerous operations and of course, my own experience in the chapel and our meeting with John at Pip' n' Jay.

Steve was a committed Christian and he was amazed at what he heard.

'I have no idea why I was prompted to go over and speak to your wife and Joanne that day and to offer to pray for you.'

We were just one family out of many in the canteen that day as far as he was concerned and Joanne was only in for a small, routine operation.

'It's amazing,' he kept saying, 'The Lord knew you all needed that prayer before any of us did. God loves and cares for us all so much.'

Sue and I were just as amazed as he was, if not more so, especially when we looked back on all that had happened.

Did it really mean God was interested in us?

Did it really mean He knew all about us? What an amazing thought.

Four months later Joanne was finally allowed to come home. It was a red letter day. The one we had all been waiting for. She was wheeled down the corridors and out into the sunshine. Sue and I helped her carefully into the car and started the short drive home. As we rounded the corner at the bottom of our road we were faced with an amazing sight. The whole family were there, standing on the roundabout, cheering and waving a big banner with "WELCOME HOME JOANNE!" written across it.

Everyone came back to the caravan and there were presents for Joanne and lots of hugs and cups of coffee, tea and cakes. Joanne had her head fixed in a huge metal halo frame, which would be with her for months to come. She stood up amidst all the happy chatter and announced, 'I just want to play this song to you all, 'cos this is how I feel about you all, my family.' She switched on the tape. It was 'Because You Loved Me' by Celine Dion.

As we listened to the words of the song, Sue and I looked at each other. This was exactly how we felt God had been to us through all those dark and terrible times. We reached over and hugged each other. We were so hopeful and filled with thanks.

Chapter 11

A WHOLE NEW WORLD

We were beginning to settle down into a normal routine; normal for us, that is. Joanne needed a lot of home nursing, but as the months went on she was able to become more independent and grew stronger each day. Her metal head halo stayed on for several months. It was really difficult to live with, and even more difficult to sleep in, but Joanne was a fighter like me and an optimist like her mother, and she more than survived. She amazed us all with her attitude and ability to stay cheerful under such conditions. However, it was hard for us, as her parents, to see her living with pain and to think of the long-term effects that could be down the line for her.

Our family were fantastic and came over to help her a lot. There were other visitors too, including Steve whom we had met in the hospital canteen.

'Why don't you come to our church?' Steve said one day. 'We have a coffee morning every Thursday.'

We politely turned him down. We were Gypsies and Gypsies didn't go to coffee mornings. *I don't want to be messing about with all that*, I thought, *they're all well-spoken at those places*. I didn't feel like I could ever be a part of something like that. I didn't want to offend Steve, so my response was, 'We probably will.'

But in November 1999 we did eventually go for coffee. We felt we needed someone to talk to because I knew there was a God and I couldn't understand what was happening to me. We went a couple of times for coffee and chatted to a few people. They seemed OK; at least they weren't throwing the Bible at us. Meanwhile, in spite of all that had happened, I was still getting drunk and smoking cannabis.

Not long after that, Steve said to me, 'Larry, why don't you come to one of our evening church services? It's quieter than the morning one.'

Uh-oh, here we go, I thought. *Bible bashing.*

Then Steve said something that changed my mind.

'Larry, why don't you sacrifice something for God? He's done so much for you.'

That stopped me in my tracks. Sunday and Thursday evenings were my God. I used to drink ten to fourteen pints and get stoned but I really thought about what Steve had said.

'I will give up Sunday night out of respect for what He has done for Joanne.' I decided.

When the Sunday evening arrived, Sue and I were really anxious. We got ready and got into the car, but it wouldn't start. It had never done that before. But we had promised Steve we would be there, so we tried and tried until at last, the car spluttered into life. We arrived just in time.

We walked into The Sanctuary Church in Staple Hill, Bristol and loads of people came over to shake our hands. We were very moved by what a warm and friendly place it was. I had expected there to be an organ as I'd been to hundreds of funerals when I was a boy and to me, the organ represented death. There was no organ but there were people singing and clapping, and there was a little band on stage with guitars and a drum kit. I couldn't believe people were shaking hands with me, a Traveller, and they even seemed to like me. In the pub some people hated me.

At the end of the service, the pastor stood up.

'Is there anyone here who would like to become a Christian?' he asked.

Before this, I'd been looking at my watch and trying to work out if I still had time to go to the pub. The next thing I knew, I was walking to the front of the church and Sue was next to me.

The pastor and his assistant took Sue and I into another room and talked to us. They talked about what we wanted and asked us how we were feeling. Then they asked if they could pray with us. We said yes and we talked out loud to God about the things we had done in our lives so far and how sorry we were for them. We told God that we wanted a second chance. I knew God and Jesus were real by now and I wanted to know God much better. From now on I wanted to live by His rules. Not mine.

Sue and I left the room feeling relieved and on a high. I was absolutely buzzing. It was a fantastic feeling. On our way out, everyone shook hands with us and we left the church in a daze. On the way home, we passed the pub where I usually went on Sundays.

'You know what?' I said to Sue. 'I've got a better feeling coming out of that church than I've ever had coming out of the pub.'

Sue and I came home that Sunday evening full of the things we'd seen and heard. We were touched by the fact that we had been accepted by the people in the church. As Gypsies, we were not used to being accepted. In fact, straight after the service, as everyone was chatting, drinking coffee and eating donuts, we began to really feel how warm and friendly everyone was.

Out of church it was a different picture. Some of the people in the community who knew me thought I was involved in some sort of scam when they found out I had been going to church. Larry Harvey going to church? My reputation may have gone before me but these churchgoers were just about the only people who were prepared to see a new side to me. The pastor had even said that God loved everybody, no matter where they came from, who they were or what they had done. Did that really mean me as well?

But when I was back at home eating my Sunday roast, I began to wonder what I'd done. I thought of all the things I wouldn't be able to do anymore. I wasn't going to be able to fight, or get drunk, or steal caravans, or pass on false papers, or do any of the things I'd been doing up until that point to make money and get thrills. *Oh help.* This wasn't like me at all. I was usually out drinking and fighting. Yet here I was, going to church and saying prayers with a pastor. I was even starting to feel like I didn't want my old way of life anymore. What had happened to me? What had I done? I was in a state of shock and later, I told the pastor how I felt.

'One day at a time Larry,' he said, 'Take it one day at a time.'

'But I'm from a Traveller background. I've been persecuted and treated as an outcast from society all my life. Why would God care about me?'

'It doesn't matter what culture we come from, or what colour we are, ' my pastor said, 'No matter where we live or what we've done, God really does know and love each and every one of us, and he loves you, Larry, as much as anyone else.'

That was an idea that was really hard for me to understand, let alone accept. I felt that it was impossible because of who I was, but we still went to church every Sunday morning and evening from then on.

It was the first time in my life that I was mixing with people who weren't Gypsies but who accepted us as equals, no questions asked. For the first time in my life I didn't feel like people hated me or looked down on me. And it was the first time in my life I felt safe and not in danger of being hurt by people.

Sue and I got so much out of the Sunday services that later on we agreed to go to a Bible Study. This consisted of a few other people from the church who met in someone's house one evening each week. Over a cup of coffee and a piece of cake, we would study the Bible together for a couple of hours and find out how God meant us to live. We would discuss what He had to say on almost every subject you could imagine. It was exciting and new and we had a lot to learn. There was so much help in the Bible that we had never realized was there. I still couldn't quite believe what was happening to me. I was someone from a Gypsy family who was sitting in a home with a crowd of people who were non-Gypsies. I stuck with it because I knew I had had an experience of God. It gave me a buzz that I never got from any illegal drug or drink.

As well as going to the Bible Study, I read the Bible for six months, every evening before I went to sleep. I was desperate to know as much of it as I could and I was amazed by what I could learn. It made so much sense now, whereas I hadn't ever understood a word of it when I'd tried to read it before. My personal experience when God spoke to me in the chapel had changed everything.

But it wasn't all plain sailing. Reading didn't come easily to me and there were other problems too. I read the Bible every evening for those six months but then for the next four months, it was like a battle. In the morning, when I opened my eyes it would be like a voice in my head was saying, 'You're wasting your time with this. You'll live to the end of it and then there'll be nothing.' I had to shake my head and try to ignore that voice. I prayed, talked to the pastor and just tried to keep going, but it wasn't easy. I had many of those disturbing thoughts going through my head throughout that time.

During those difficult times, I would often be in church on a Sunday, singing hymns with everyone else there and I would suddenly think, *what am I doing here?* Then I would look down at my watch and think, *normally at this time of day I'd be stoned on cannabis.* For a Traveller, churches were for funerals, not for getting to know God and certainly not for having a good time. Even as these things were racing around in my head, I would realize that I really liked the happiness and the peace I found in the church. The people were so friendly there and it was much better than anything I had ever found in the pub.

For Sue and me, the struggles continued. We had a lot on our minds; our past, our drug-taking, our way of life. We wanted to get it all off our chests, so we summoned up our courage and went to talk to the pastor. We were really scared of what he would think and whether he would want anything else to do with us. But he wasn't shocked, just pleased we had been brave enough to share it with him. Instead of sending us away in disgust, he was thrilled that we had come to learn about God and he wanted to pray for us, for help in our future to put the past behind us.

We were surprised and relieved by his reaction, but then most things that happened that summer were a surprise to us. It was a whole new world and we had no idea what the future was going to hold for us. Perhaps it was just as well we didn't.

Chapter 12

THE WOMAN IN WHITE

The months passed and Joanne, 18 years old now, was still wearing the metal frame which was keeping her bones and metal plates in place while they knitted together. She had to go to the hospital every two weeks to have it tightened and she had to be so careful not to damage it or hurt herself. Each night, she needed to be helped into bed and she could only sleep sitting up. She could not put any clothes on over her head, so one of her friends made her lots of sleeveless tops in different colours, fastened with Velcro so that she could put them on easily. She couldn't have a proper shower and had to bathe without getting her head wet.

During this time, Sue was Joanne's main carer. She washed her, dressed her and brushed her hair. It was all the reward she needed just to have Joanne there with her. I was so thankful for simple things we could do together at that time, like watching our favourite TV show, *Only Fools and Horses*. I thanked God I was able to do that with my little girl. I thanked God she was at home.

When Joanne was well enough to go shopping, there were times when she would walk into a supermarket and the place would come to a standstill. It seemed like everyone was looking at her. We would often hear people saying, 'Oh, look at that poor girl.' Joanne's response would be, 'Don't worry about it, I'm not a "poor girl!"'

When she had seen the impact that knowing Jesus had made in our lives, Joanne had become a Christian too. She was so amazed at how different her parents' lives were now, that she had begun to experience knowing that God was in charge of her own life too.

And at last the happy time came when she could finally be free of her frame. It had been a triumph of Joanne's will that she had been so patient through all the long months. When the frame was finally taken off though, her troubles weren't over. She had to get used to not having the extra weight on her shoulders and this made her very dizzy. Her balance was off for a while, until she got used to it. Gradually life was at last getting back to normal for Joanne and the rest of us.

I went back to work and Sue kept things smoothly ticking along at home. Everything was beginning to look very promising.

A year of peace followed, until we began to notice that Joanne was falling asleep again at odd times. It got so bad that in January 2000 we called the doctor.

'Right,' he said immediately. 'Go straight back to Ward Two.'

We all drove together to Frenchay Hospital and walked into the Neurological Ward. It was not good to be back and all sorts of thoughts were racing through our minds. The hospital staff checked Joanne's oxygen levels. They were very low, at about 48 per cent. The duty consultant came to see us and explained that Joanne would need to be admitted immediately. *Here we go again,* I thought. We were dreading what might happen next.

Joanne was admitted to the ward and was examined by her surgeon, Mr Bolger, who organized an immediate scan down in radiology. Back on the ward, with the results in, he made his way over to Sue and me, took a deep breath and looked at us.

'There are a few problems which have occurred.'

'Is she going to be alright?' I asked.

'I don't know.'

Mr Bolger explained what he had seen on the scan.

'One of the metal rods which has been put into Joanne's neck to support her head, has developed a 5-millimetre kink. This means it isn't working properly and is causing pressure on her brainstem, which in turn is causing her to fall asleep again.'

We groaned and prepared for what was coming next.

'Joanne will need another ten-hour operation.'

We had to accept it and once again went through the agony of waiting, but this time we were able to pray together, knowing that God was in charge.

When the wait was over, the results came back and they were not the results for which we had longed and prayed.

Joanne's operation had not worked.

Mr Bolger came to give us the news and explain what had happened.

'We are going to have to put Joanne back on the halo.'

The halo was the head frame Joanne had had to wear for so long before.

'We need to do this right away in order to raise her head up from her spine. Then we'll need to operate again in three weeks' time and put her on this gadget.'

The gadget in question was designed to try and raise Joanne's head above her spine by stretching two wires from the halo down over the back of the bed and attaching weights to the wires to pull her head upwards.

Each night they would check Joanne using a scan and each time

Mr Bolger would report, 'It needs just a little more time, but we're getting there.'

After some time, Joanne was ready for her next operation, but there was another problem. It was cancelled several times. On one occasion, Mr Bolger had flown back from a visit to Ireland, only to find the operation had been cancelled yet again. We were told there was no funding for the titanium needed for the rod inserts. We were devastated.

Our pastor, Darren, had been a constant source of support to us through all the tough times. During these testing moments, he felt he had been given a verse from the Bible especially for the family. It came from the Old Testament, 1 Kings chapter 18, and was the story of Elijah who sent his servant out to look for a rain cloud during a drought. It was only on the seventh time that the servant was able to see the promised cloud, which was the sign that rain and relief from the drought was on the way.

'This story is for you,' he said. 'Although the operation keeps being cancelled, on the seventh time it will go ahead and when it does, it will be in God's perfect timing. Just as the rain cloud had come at the perfect time, so will the operation for Joanne.'

After six cancellations, Joanne's operation finally happened on the seventh attempt.

And it lasted for eleven agonizing hours.

The surgeons put another rod next to the faulty one to solve the problem. Throughout the long hours of each operation, Sue and I were praying, along with our entire church. All along we both felt the presence of God with us. It was a huge comfort.

Joanne had her 19th birthday in intensive care. She lay in her hospital bed, surrounded by flowers, presents and balloons. Whilst we were chatting to her, Sue noticed that her pillow was wet and that she was also a bit sleepy. She reported it to the nurse.

'Well, she has just had an operation,' the nurse replied.

But Sue knew this wasn't normal. She insisted something was wrong and eventually the nurses checked Joanne's blood gasses, only to find they were all over the place. Mr Bolger was called. He looked at all the balloons and cards and then smiled.

'Happy Birthday Joanne.'

Then his face changed.

'I am so sorry to have to tell you that we've got to take you back into surgery immediately. Time is of the essence.'

He took Sue and I aside and explained what had happened.

'We must have pierced the brain sac. If too much cerebrospinal fluid leaks out, the brain will sink. If it sinks too far and sticks to the scar tissue, it will be devastating. We have to act fast.'

Within an hour they had prepared Joanne for another op and she was once again wheeled down into the operating suite. Sue always went with her into the anaesthetist's room. Usually I couldn't face being there, but this time, because Sue had always felt the calming and loving presence of God with her in the room, I felt brave enough to go too. I followed Sue and the trolley down the long corridor, and into the neurosurgical operating theatre.

It took a long time to put Joanne out, as she had to have a special procedure, known as 'the fibre optic awake procedure'. This meant that she was given sedation and was put onto the life support equipment before being anaesthetized. This took over an hour and as it was happening, Sue and I watched in panic as our daughter's blood pressure and oxygen levels started to drop dramatically - 60 over 40 and still dropping - normal blood pressure is around 120 over 80.

Joanne was going into shock.

Sue panicked, 'It's dropping.'

The ICU nurse took hold of her hand.

'It's alright. It's going to be alright.'

We watched helplessly as the anaesthetist, his assistant and the theatre nurse, all dressed in green, busied themselves to right this life-or-death situation. There was tension in the air and they worked quickly and silently to save Joanne's life.

As we watched on, we both saw another nurse in a white uniform standing just behind Joanne's head. She was smiling and looking directly at Joanne.

Sue thought, "That nurse is praying for our Joanne."

I couldn't bear the tension any longer.

I ran out of the room to join the rest of the family and we all waited at the top of the corridor.

Sue stayed in the room.

'Please God,' she prayed. 'Don't let her die.'

At that moment, the nurse in white stepped forward to where Joanne's head was, put her hands on Joanne's shoulders and looked up, her mouth moving quietly as she did so.

Sue cried out again.

'Please Lord, don't let her die.'

At that instant, all the machines registered Joanne's vital levels as normal.

There was a huge air of relief in the room.

The anaesthetist, a tall man with a big white beard, was sweating now but he began to to guide the fibre optic equipment into Joanne's lungs.

'Right, we're in,' he said. 'Let's go.'

With that, they quickly wheeled Joanne out of the room and straight into the operating theatre.

The rest of the team relaxed and the ICU nurse put her arm on Sue's shoulder.

'Come on,' she said. 'She'll be alright now.'

Sue was physically and emotionally drained, but all she could think of was the nurse in white.

'Who was that nurse in white standing at our Joanne's head?' she asked the nurse. 'Do you think she was praying for her?'

'Nurse in white?' the nurse exclaimed. 'There was nobody in there dressed in white. None of us wear white in this hospital.'

Sue was shocked.

'You're telling me you didn't see her?'

The nurse looked at Sue and put her arm around her.

'Sue, you've had a nasty shock. Come back to the ward with me and I'll make you a nice hot cup of tea.'

As Sue walked along the corridor with the nurse, she asked again about the woman in white and again the nurse patted her arm and insisted that there had been no one dressed like that in the room. She was worried about Sue and was certain that she was in a state of profound shock and didn't know what she was talking about.

Sue walked into the waiting room where I was sitting, along with the rest of the family. I jumped up as soon as she came in.

'Sue, is Joanne alright?' I couldn't bear to wait any longer.

'She's alright Larry,' Sue said and we hugged each other, so relieved.

'Larry, did you see that nurse in the operating theatre with Joanne?'

'Do you mean the one in white behind her?'

'You saw her too! I'm not going mad after all. I have to find out who she is.'

The ICU nurse took a deep breath. 'There was no one in white,' she repeated. 'We only have physios dressed in white uniform, but they have blue piping round their sleeves and neck and they certainly don't come into that room.' She shrugged her shoulders and turned to Sue. 'I'll make you that cup of tea,' she said and she hurried from the room.

The mystery remained and it was all Sue could think about. The nurse in white had made a huge impression on both of us. She had such a lovely face and an air of calm throughout the whole crisis.

Later that day our pastor came to the hospital as he did most days.

'What you witnessed in the operating theatre,' he said, 'could only have been an angel, sent at exactly the right moment for Joanne.'

Sue knew that the Lord had been looking after them that day. She hurried into Joanne's ward to tell her all about it. By then Joanne was a great believer. She loved to sing the song, 'Jesus loves me, this I know, for the Bible tells me so,' and for her, this just confirmed the words of that simple but profound verse.

Chapter 13

A VERY SPECIAL COAT

Through all of this, we had a strong sense of the presence of God. In the months that followed, it provided us with comfort throughout the many medical procedures and helped us to support Joanne as she got back onto her feet. From Intensive Care, she went onto the High Dependency Ward whilst we waited for the results of the latest scan to see if the operation had been successful.

One Saturday, Sue and I were sitting by Joanne's bed. I was looking down at the floor and noticed a pair of old trainers and jeans come into view. It was Mr Bolger, who had come in on his day off to see how Joanne was doing. He was as thrilled as we were that she was doing so well.

Some weeks later, Sue was walking down the long hospital corridor when she spotted the anaesthetist who had been attending to Joanne on the day her vital signs had crashed. Sue plucked up courage to stop him.

'I'm sorry to stop you and you probably don't know me, but...'

'Yes, I do,' he said, 'you're Joanne's mum, aren't you?'

'Yes, I am. I just wanted to ask you if you noticed a nurse dressed in white that day in the theatre? She was standing behind her head and I think she was praying for our Joanne.'

'A nurse in white?'

'Yes.'

'Really?'

Sue insisted.

'Well, as far as I know there was no-one in white that day, but I believe you. It's not the first time I've heard something like this.'

He went on to tell Sue that he'd been told of similar stories in the past, 'always when young people were involved and always when it was a life or death situation.'

Before Joanne was allowed to leave the hospital, her breathing had to stabilize. The initial compression of her brainstem had left her with some breathing difficulties when she went to sleep. This meant she had to be moved to another hospital, to a bed in the specialized Respiratory Ward at the Bristol Royal Infirmary. She would need to be there for six weeks.

Joanne had already spent four months in Frenchay Hospital by this time and as a family we were so grateful for how she was looked after. The doctors, nurses and all the staff had taken Joanne to their hearts and the way they cared for her was fantastic.

With this in mind, we were worried about her having to move to another hospital where nobody knew us. We mentioned this to Darren, our Pastor, who said, 'We'll pray for her before she leaves and we'll pray that God provides Christian nurses and doctors to be with her.' So we all prayed and we all expected the Lord to answer.

However, it didn't seem as if He had answered this time. When we finally arrived at the Bristol Royal Infirmary by ambulance, Joanne was wheeled into a depressingly dark, old-fashioned ward that frankly we all thought was horrible. As we came into the room, a nurse was busy by Joanne's bed, cleaning the ward. Sue noticed that her name badge read Godfrieda. Then the consultant, Dr C-, came in to see us. We began to talk to him about Joanne. After a few minutes, Sue stopped the conversation and said, 'Excuse me for asking, but are you a Christian Dr C-?'

'Yes, I am.'

The nurse, Godfrieda, stopped what she was doing, looked up and turned to us. 'I am a Christian too!' she said.

This was the answer to our prayers. The care Joanne received from Godfrieda and Dr C- could not have been better or more professional. God had heard our prayers and supplied our every need. As Sue said, 'What we prayed for, because it was God's will, we expected.'

In spite of all the terrible medical procedures Joanne had had to endure, her faith had increased tenfold as she witnessed answers to her prayers. Throughout it all, none of us ever felt that God had let us down in any way. On the harder days, Darren would comfort us and say, 'Listen to me, what God has started, God will finish. He has it all in His hands. You are not to worry.' When Joanne's life was threatened, as it was so many times, he would say, 'God would not have brought her this far and brought you, a beautiful family, this far, to drop you all now.'

It was true. Sue and I were in awe at how God showed how much He cared for us and loved us through it all. We thought God was amazing. Everywhere we went, we told our story of how good God had been to us and Joanne. Every Sunday morning, we went to church and read our Bibles. After church, we went back to our situation in the hospital, and we knew the Lord was with us.

Darren kept the church folk up to date with how Joanne was doing and would say, 'These people astound me. They spend hours and hours at the hospital and then they're back here to praise the Lord and dance.' It seemed like God was touching the whole church, not just our family.

On the great day that Joanne was due to leave the hospital, I put a coat over her shoulders, ready for the journey. This was not just any old coat, this was a special coat. I had bought it for Joanne when she went into hospital the second time. I had always told myself that Joanne would be well enough to wear it one day. I had believed that one day she would put on that coat and go home. That day had finally arrived.

Chapter 14

BACK TO PRISON AGAIN

By this time, Darren our Pastor, had suggested we might like to get married, something we hadn't thought of before! Sue and I agreed it was a good next step to be honouring to God and so I went off to the Mall to pick the rings.

It wasn't a big affair. Just me, Sue and the kids. We all went off to Yate Registry Office, Sue in a powder blue trouser suit and me in a smart shirt and trousers. I was really emotional during the ceremony. I kept thinking how blessed we were to have our five children with us as witnesses, and not four as could so easily have happened. Sue had to keep lending me her handkerchief!

The children thought it was all wonderful. We had never seen it as important before, but they sensed the closeness we had as a unit now and could see how our lives had begun to change. They saw it in the way we spoke to each other and in the way we now dealt with things. It was all so different, nothing was a huge problem any more and we relied on God for everything. The children could see all that and it put them at ease.

It felt right to us too, because God had done so much for us and we felt it was the next step to putting thing right before God. It was important to us to honour Him in that way.

After the very short ceremony we took ourselves off for our first meal as a married couple, in the local pub with all the kids. It was a great day! Another fresh start!

So Sue and I were going from strength to strength in our new life and we had made many new friends at church. Simon and his wife Jane were amongst those friends. Exciting things were happening. Simon and I, along with a group from the church, signed up to go on a missionary trip to Ukraine. It was to be the first of five trips I would make there.

This first time we went, we had to catch two flights and then it was thirty hours on a train across rough open countryside. With an interpreter I told my life story for the first time in a rehab centre in front of one hundred men and women. When I had finished, a Ukrainian man came to speak to me.

'I lost everything due to drugs,' he said through the interpreter, 'But I became a Christian and God gave me back my family, my home, and my market business.'

He then presented a watch to me.

'I liked your story so much I want you to have this. It belonged to my late father.'

I backed away, I didn't want to take it, but I soon realised that it was disrespectful to refuse his gift. It meant so much to him. I learned a lot about Ukrainian culture in that place and came to admire the people tremendously.

The folk in the village where we stayed didn't have many possessions but they got up every morning at 6:30 to pray for food for the day. Whilst we were there, we prayed with them. These people were so poor but they had a contentment in their lives and were very close to God. While we were there, I managed to give the pastor a gift of 400 dollars to buy a bungalow with an acre of land. This was going to be turned into somewhere ex-criminals and prostitutes could live off the land, growing and selling their own produce. They were amazing people and it was a wonderful experience.

Back home, instead of dealing with the underworld as we had done in the past, we gave up all our illegal doings and earned our living legally through demolition and scrap metal. I gave up drugs and heavy drinking. It was a huge relief and a huge change - for the better!

Later on Sue and I talked about it and prayed and decided that we would start raising money for Frenchay Hospital, as a thank you to them for saving Joanne's life and being so fantastic with our entire family. Our aim was to raise £10,000 to buy new equipment for the Brain Injury Unit. We decided the best way to raise the money would be to travel around pubs and garages and ask if they could put sweet jars on the counters to collect money from passing customers. We auctioned gifts donated by local sportsmen from the Empire Sports Club and we bought raffle tickets and sold them to our family and friends.

One of my good friends, Malcolm, was a boxing promoter. He took me to Manchester to watch a boxing show and introduced me to Thomas 'Hit Man' Hearns at the end of the show. Malcolm took me backstage to the dressing rooms and I managed to get a pair of new boxing gloves signed by Mr Hearns. I was also able to pray with him after I had shared Joanne's story with him. After that, the boxing gloves travelled all over the country and were signed by fifteen world boxing champions. Not long after that, we surpassed our target of £10,000. We managed to raise a total of £13,500.

When the money was all in and counted, I picked up the phone and called Mr Sandeman, the brain surgeon in the Unit, and told him we wanted to give him the cheque. When he heard how much money we had raised, he was amazed and delighted.

'I can't believe this, Larry. We were just discussing how we were going to raise £10,000 for a piece of equipment we need that measures the swelling of the brain!'

The staff in the unit were delighted to accept the cheque, and the remaining £3,500 went to the ICU.

Life at home had changed as well. I began to think about how I could help boys who were in similar situations to those I had been in; boys who were making bad choices and getting into trouble. I had hated being in prison and now I had this different perspective on life, I wanted to give something back. I started to pray about it and called all my contacts, trying to find out how I could get into prisons to help the lads there.

My answer came in the form of a man called Ryan, who happened to go to the Empire Sports Club. Ryan volunteered in Ashfield, a local modern Young Offenders Institution (YOI) for boys from ages 15 to 18. Ashfield was situated only a couple of miles up the road from my home. I was intrigued when Ryan said he was going to a local church the next evening to hear the Revd Nick Hay, the chaplain from Ashfield, speak about his work in the prison. I jumped at the chance to join him. I had no idea that this was going to be another life-changing moment for me.

The Revd Hay had wild hair which stuck up above his cheeky face. He had a wicked sense of humour and when he wasn't in Ashfield, he played the electric guitar in a rock band. I immediately liked what I saw and loved even more what I heard from Nick. As soon as he began to speak, I knew the message was for me. I had never heard anyone talk like this man and so much of what he was saying was new to me. I was captivated. Here was a modern-day vicar, talking about prison and prisoners like he really knew and cared about them. Not only that, he expected God to work in their lives. This was far from the 'funeral type' vicar I was used to. He was amazing. I knew that talking to those lads in prison could and did make a difference and I wanted to help. Something told me that this was right for me.

I approached Nick straight after the meeting.

I told him a bit about my background. 'I'd like to talk to the lads about what has happened to me. Can I go into Ashfield and speak to them? I know what they've been through. I've been there. I understand them and I know I can help them.'

Nick listened to everything I had to say and seemed impressed. He agreed it would be great if I could speak to the lads but warned me it wasn't going to be easy, especially with my record. He promised he would help as much as he could, but stressed that prisons have strict policies regarding who they allow to come in and with my past record it was probably going to be impossible.

All of my life I had been trying to stay out of prison. Now, all I wanted to do was get back in! But that was easier said than done. It was so frustrating. First, I had to apply for a CRB (Criminal Records Bureau) certificate. Everyone who wants to have contact with prisoners on an official basis needs to be checked for any criminal record. This gives people access to all your files, criminal and otherwise. There was a lot of security paperwork to get through, with long and complicated forms to be filled out. My heart sank. The odds were not in my favour. With my criminal record, it would be almost impossible for me to receive a CRB certificate.

However, Nick posted the forms to me anyway and I filled them in with Sue's help. It was tempting not to mention my twenty-seven convictions and to omit details of my stay in the YOI, my time in prison, my probation periods and all of my overnight stays in Police cells. But I couldn't do that. I filled in all the forms honestly. What else could I do?

It was now up to God. If He wanted me in that prison to help the boys, then I would get the certificate. Even so, I had very little hope. I prayed, posted the forms and waited. And waited and waited. Months passed, until one day I was in my dad's scrapyard when a call came through for me. It was Nick.

'It must be God, Larry. They're talking about letting you in! Can you come into Ashfield next week for a chat?'

I couldn't believe it, and neither could Nick. This was a chance in a million.

I put on my best suit, slicked down my hair and went off to

meet Nick. I was so used to being on the other side of the fence for all my previous prison visits, I was gobsmacked to be greeted so politely by the guards at reception. They led me like an honoured guest through a series of huge, locked, clanging iron gates and I was escorted by a prison officer across two prison yards, up a metal staircase and into the chaplaincy. It felt strange to be treated so respectfully and to pass by the lads in their green sweatshirts, staring at me and wondering who I was. Little did they know, only a few years before that, I had been one of them.

When I arrived at Nick's office, just outside the chapel, he greeted me with a grin.

'You've made it then Larry.'

He showed me round the chaplaincy offices and into the airy, modern chapel. There was a large painting of the Prodigal Son on the wall above the altar, falling into the arms of his father (Luke 15). Nick explained that there were about 400 boys in the prison, either in a cell by themselves, or sharing a cell if they had earned enough privileges to be with a friend.

He took me out to see the wings and the rest of the prison. I was impressed. It was very different from my days in Eastwood Park. There was a toilet and sink in each room. There were music centres and televisions. The doors were left open and for five hours a day the boys went to lessons in a separate education wing. The staff all seemed highly motivated and in most cases they treated the boys with a humorous, light touch, and the boys responded in a similar vein. I liked what I was seeing.

Two months after that visit, I was allowed in as a volunteer. Somehow, I had been granted permission, criminal record and all. It was a miracle. Even more amazing than that, I was given my own set of keys, something I thought I would never have. I will never forget the day they handed them over to me. They weren't just the keys to some of the prison doors; they were something that would unlock a whole new way of life for me; a life without deceit or fear of capture. A life without heavy drinking, drug-taking, violence and guilt.

From then on, my friend Ryan and I visited the prison every Thursday evening to chat to the boys. Come rain or shine, the two of us did this for the next four years. The idea was to get to know the boys, find out if they had any worries or problems and help them when we could.

We played table tennis with them and we talked with anyone who wanted to chat. Sometimes one of the boys would have something on their mind and we would listen to them and give advice where we could. This all took place during the social time in the evenings when the boys were out of their rooms and could mix with each other or just sit around and have a laugh. I knew it would take time to build up relationships here but I didn't mind. Once upon a time, I had spent every Thursday in the pub getting drunk. I used to hate prisons. I hated the smell of prison and I hated the staff. Now I was going into a prison voluntarily and I was enjoying every minute.

After three-and-a-half years of faithful prison visiting, Nick called me into his office one day and hit me with a bombshell - a good one.

'Larry, how would you like to be put on staff and work as part of the chaplaincy team for two hours a week?'

He explained it could only be two hours each week because that was as much as their budget allowed, but he hoped there would be a possibility of more hours in the future. I was over the moon. I felt respected, and I was getting paid for it. I had my own tray in the office too, with my name on it. That meant a lot to me, to be trusted.

I loved the job and was getting on better and better with the lads. I could see I was making a difference in their lives. My two hours a week carried on until a few months later, when Nick's assistant, Dave asked to speak to me. True to his word, Nick had spoken to the prison governor. Dave and Nick had told her about my work with the lads, how I shared my story with them and how it touched their lives. The governor was impressed and found the money so that I could come in and work all day every Friday, in addition to my two hours. This was wonderful news for me. I felt I was at my best when speaking to the lads. My own experience was like a gift. I had had a hard time in a YOI and this meant I knew the right things to say to these boys. I was able to give them hope, something which no one had given me when I was in prison.

Time went on and in my quest to help the boys, I would sometimes become a little overenthusiastic and forget the rules. I would rush ahead without thinking and was well-known for being unorthodox, although effective.

Every Friday I had to attend a meeting where staff would review the boys and the day-to-day running of the prison. This meeting was chaired very strictly by Vicky O'Dea, the Prison Director. Vicky was hugely respected throughout the prison and she stood for no nonsense, either from the boys or her staff. She liked us all to abide by the rules and she kept me on my toes. At one of these meetings, Vicky heard about one of my outbursts to a member of staff who I thought had been unfair to one of the boys. She took me to one side.

'Just remember Larry,' she said with a wry smile, pointing to her head and to her toes, 'feet are for dancing and heads are for thinking!'

Vicky treated everyone the same and I had a lot of respect for her.

Fridays in the chaplaincy were busy days because I had to do 'the stats'. This meant that every Friday morning I attended the Induction Meeting. This was for all the new boys who had come into the prison that week. It was held in a room just off reception and each department sent someone to explain what their options and opportunities were whilst they were inside. For me, this meant introducing myself, telling them about the chaplaincy and letting them know that we were there to help. I would ask if they had any questions and reassure them that, although everything seemed new and frightening at first, they would soon settle in.

Nick and Dave then talked to the boys and explained that they could have visits from a chaplain of their faith whenever they wanted.

'It doesn't matter if you are Christian, Muslim, Buddhist or any other belief, you can just have a chat if there is anything on your mind, or you can attend the midweek Bible study sessions. You can attend religious services. Muslims use the Chapel on Fridays for their prayers and Christians can attend a service in the chapel on Sunday mornings.'

I was excited about the opportunity to talk with the boys individually. I knew there could be times when they felt afraid of what lay ahead for them. I told Nick I'd like to share my life story with them and within a couple of weeks, I was allowed to take over the chaplaincy slot at the Induction Meeting. For the next five years I gave a shortened version of my life story to the boys. It was an amazing opportunity to get their attention and believe me, I had their attention. Those talks opened hundreds of questions and conversations throughout the years and it was never challenged by the prison, even though it lay a little outside the remit of the purpose of the meeting.

After spending time with the new boys, the next task on Fridays was to visit the hospital wing. I would knock on each hospital cell door and visit every lad in the hospital wing to make sure they were OK and had everything they needed.

It was also my job to visit the lads who had misbehaved that week and been put in the special segregation block to calm them down; this was for their own protection and the protection of the other boys. In accordance with the law, each young offender in the hospital and the segregation block had to be visited daily by a member of the chaplaincy to check how they were doing, both mentally and physically. I would go through into the special wing, walk from cell to cell, and have a word with each one. I tried to find out what had caused them to act out in the first place and establish how they were feeling now. I knew the boys really well and they listened to me, but more importantly, I listened to them.

After these rounds, I would visit the general wings in different parts of the prison. I enjoyed getting to know the staff and the boys, learning their life stories and seeing where I could help with a word here or there. Being able to say, 'I've done that,' and, 'I've been where you are,' really helped me to get to know the boys. Once they knew my story, they would often stop and think about what they were doing. They asked me questions and usually asked if they could see me again. I was thrilled to be able to help them. As my reputation spread, lads would often pass me by on the football pitch and call out, 'Sir, are you that one what got in fights and was put in prison?' They were amazed that, after all I had done, I was now part of the staff team.

As I got to know the boys better, I was able to tell them what believing in Jesus had done for me and what He could do for them if they wanted to ask Him into their lives. I was never pushy with my faith, I just told my story and listened patiently to theirs. There were often many tears on both sides and a lot of whispered prayers were said in the chapel, or in a quiet corner during 'sosh.' I felt my whole life had been leading up to doing this work. I knew I was where I was meant be.

Sometimes, the boys would act as if they didn't care about being inside and pretended that they were tough and strong. This was often just a front; many of them were afraid of what prison would be like. I knew this because I had felt very frightened myself when I had to go to Eastwood Park. If you hadn't been in prison before, there was a fear of not knowing what to expect. If you had, it was *knowing* what to expect.

I built up good relationships with the boys and gained their trust. When I spoke to them quietly and in private, they would often break down in tears. Most would tell me that they wanted to change from what they were doing and live a different life once they got out. They really meant it at the time but it was different once they were outside with their mates. Many times, consuming alcohol and drugs would make them do things they would bitterly regret later. Many of the boys returned very quickly after being released. It was a real problem. And just what I had done at their age.

Inside the prison, it was buzzing with activity. I always sat down to a huge lunch in the bistro for prison staff. Just £1.50 for two courses and all cooked by the boys. If they liked you, they gave you bigger portions and my lunches were huge! It was a great way to train the boys for catering jobs once they were out of prison. However, it wasn't helping me to keep trim, so I started to drop into the gym once the meal had gone down, putting on my boxing gloves and doing a bit of training and sparring with other members of staff. Then it was back to work on the wings, taking Bible classes in the chapel, showing films to the lads and talking to them about their hopes and dreams for the future.

The education block in the prison had a great team of dedicated teachers who worked hard to make the lessons interesting for the boys. Every day the boys would walk in a long line round the edge of the football field from their cell blocks to the education block. Here they were divided into small groups of about eight boys to one teacher. The teacher always stood with their back directly to the door and there were prison officers posted outside each classroom along the corridors. Many of the lads sat GCSEs and A Levels, and these were often boys who had been poor attenders and poor readers in their school days. Many of them passed exams for the first time in their lives. It was an exciting place to be and I loved every minute of it.

One time, there was a group of lads who had extra trouble settling in. These boys were very close to my heart. They were fellow Travellers. I knew the Travellers who came into the prison had different needs from the others. Due to their lifestyle outside prison, they found it much more difficult to settle and to be confined in such a small space. Their lives had been so much freer than most of the other lads and they missed the close community they had with their extended families and fellow Travellers. Consequently, they tended to get into a lot of trouble and fights in prison. I was desperate to help them but what could I do?

I decided to ask Vicky if I could start a group just for them. I suggested I could gather the Irish and English Travellers together to talk through their problems and let them share their experiences. They could meet once a week in the chapel on Mondays when there was a free slot and I could lead it. Vicky thought it was a great idea. It would help the boys settle in and thus avoid fights and confrontations within the prison. It would benefit everyone, not just the Travellers. Vicky gave the go-ahead, and permission for me to work on Mondays as well as Fridays!

The Gypsy and Travellers' group met every Monday morning from 10:30 to 12:00 in the chapel. They were an excitable bunch and it was often hard to get them to settle down and listen. However, they respected me and I respected them. I knew their way of life and how their minds worked. Consequently, I had a good touch with them and it wasn't long until the chapel was quiet and they began to listen. I showed them DVDs on Travellers' lives and taught them to be proud of their history, their way of life and most importantly, themselves. I tried to show them that they were just as good as anyone else and reminded them that there were fewer Gypsies and Travellers in prison than any other ethnic group.

Within a few months this group were all on 'Gold Regime', the top level of good behaviour in the prison. My colleagues respected what was going on and I was voted employee of the month twice, an achievement that made me very proud.

During this period, I was going through a difficult time in my personal life. Both my mother and father passed away within four months of each other. Before that, my sister, my three brothers and myself had looked after my mum for two-and-a-half years in her own home. We each took it in turns to sleep in a bed next to her when she was very ill and we were all there the morning she died.

Soon after that, I was sharing my story with a group of unruly lads and I showed them a picture of my mum and dad.

It was too difficult for me and I broke down in front of the boys, tears streaming down my face.

Without any hesitation, every one of those boys stood up from their seats, walked over to me and put their arms around me.

It was a moment I'll never forget.

I told them how I remembered sitting with my mum when she was ill.

'I am so sorry, Mum, for being a bad boy when I was young,' I said.

'Don't worry about it,' she replied. She had forgiven me all the heartache I'd brought on her and dad because I was her son and she loved me.

This is what I would tell some of the boys whenever I would take them to the chapel to light a candle and say some prayers in memory of the death of someone close to them. They were often sorry that they hadn't had a chance to say sorry to their mum and dad or gran.

'It's true your mum or dad would not have liked you being in prison, but that would not stop them loving you. And God is like that too – His love is unconditional. Yes, God wants a better life for you, but He still loves you even though you are in prison.'

Because I got to know the boys and members of staff so well, some even asked me to conduct funeral services for them when a family member passed away and I was honoured to be able do so.

One day, after one such funeral, a member of Bristol City Council approached me in the church. He asked if I would be willing to give a presentation to the Council about my work with Gypsies inside the prison. I really wanted to help non travelling folk know how we Travellers lived and so I put together a presentation about our lives and traditions, explaining the unique problems we Travellers face in the modern world today.

From then on, invitations to speak came thick and fast. Vicky asked me to speak to the new prison staff because they needed to understand the background of these lads to get the best out of them. Who better to do that than me? I was thrilled. All I wanted was to make a difference for these boys. They were exactly like I had been when I was their age. I longed to help them to avoid the mistakes I had made and to let them know that Christ could change their lives, just as He had done for me and for Sue.

Not long after this, Vicky left us to take up a higher position and we were all sad to see her go. Her place was taken by Brian Anderson. A man after my own heart, Brian was a British Champion boxer. We got on like a house on fire.

It was a new chapter in prison life for me.

Chapter 15

A BONNY LIFE

Back at home, with Joanne out of hospital, we all settled into a life that no longer required Sue and I to rush to hospital and organize childcare, amongst other tasks like going to work, cooking, playing with the children and going to church.

On the days when I wasn't at the prison, I continued to run my own business, collecting and recycling scrap metal. I was still working in Ashfield two days a week and loving it. I was still praying that I would be given more hours. This was the job for which I felt I had been made; talking to the boys and helping them to make good decisions, instead of the bad ones I had made when I had been their age. I enjoyed helping them to see they were loved by God and could make something of their lives, that if they really wanted to, it wasn't too late for them to change. I knew that with God's help, they could do something spectacular.

It was time for me to take stock. What did I really want for my life? Was it time for a change? I thought back to how, as a child, I had always loved animals – horses in particular. How happy I had been when I was with them, riding them through the fields and simply being with them in the stables. I loved the smell of the hay and the wonderful scent of the ponies. I decided to visit some friends who bred horses. That day, I arrived back home with Bonny.

Bonny was a beautiful piebald horse with big velvet eyes.

I gently led her out of the horsebox and through the gate into her new home, a pasture which I had bought near our home. I took off her halter and patted her neck. After sniffing the air for a few seconds, Bonny lifted her head and set off at a gallop round the field; she was free. Bonny soon learned to come to me whenever I called. She followed me trustingly into her warm, cosy stable each night and every morning I got up at 6, drove down to the field, fed her and spent time with her. Those moments were precious.

One winter morning, when I arrived, it wasn't just Bonny I found in the stable. Lying by her side was a newborn, spindly, wobbly foal. I named her little Queenie. It was a lovely sight. Every morning, I cleared the frost off the car windows, put on my warmest coat and drove down to feed Bonny and little Queenie. In the summer, I would stroll down to see them early each morning. I would simply sit with them, breathing in the country air and enjoying the meadow and the stream that ran through it. This was a really special time for me, I felt so calm and peaceful when I was there.

After this, I would walk home, change my clothes and drive straight to Ashfield, to a very different world. I said 'hello' to my colleagues in reception, unlocked the doors through to the courtyards and the doors to the stairs, and made my way to the chapel complex. As I was always the first one to arrive, I would unlock all the doors in the chapel area, respond to some emails and make myself a coffee. Then, I would head over to the wings to talk to each lad I needed to see that morning. It was important I was there early in the morning because the lads went to their lessons at 8.30 and before that they were having breakfast. Unless I could get there in time to sit down and have breakfast with them, there wasn't much opportunity to have a good chat with them until the evening and 'sosh'.

I've always been a 'no nonsense' person. There were times I didn't agree with the lads, but if I could see they were hurting, all I wanted to do was help. I was uniquely positioned to be able to help the boys because I had been where they were and I remembered how it felt. I had had good parents, they just couldn't do anything with me. When I was a boy, I was totally out of control. Yet here I was in Ashfield prison, in my little office, surrounded by letters from ex-offenders and with my two Employee of the Month Certificates on the wall.

I had come a long way, but it didn't mean I had forgotten how it felt. When you're in that kind of situation you learn to accept it as normal, your unhappiness becomes a part of everyday life. However, when you have a real encounter with God and He becomes real to you, the bubble that you have been living in bursts and suddenly you are on the outside looking in on it all. You begin to see things differently when you have God in your life and you are able to deal with things you would never have been able to deal with before.

I would talk to the boys about their hopes and dreams for the future. Sometimes, they didn't have any because they were so caught up in their lifestyles. In these cases, I would encourage them to understand it was OK for them to dream and to hope for the future.

'Pride can get in the way,' I would say. 'It's a two-way thing between you and God. God does His part, but you've got to do your part too. You've got to try and God will do His part. It's all in God's timing, not yours.'

The boys would listen and ask me to pray with them, which I was more than happy to do. They were often worried about their mums or their sisters and I would pray that they would be kept safe. If their mums were poorly, which they often were, I prayed that they would get better. I often offered to call their mums to reassure them that their son was OK. This not only reassured mum, but it often calmed the boy down, knowing that his mum knew he was coping with prison life.

A big part of my role was to try to encourage the lads. I often told them, 'If your prayers aren't answered, it could be because you're still clinging to your old way of life. If you can ask Jesus to forgive you, you can start a new life. I know it's difficult to change when you go home, but you can do it if you really mean it and if you pray and read God's Word.'

Almost all the boys wanted to change. Lots of them would say things like, 'I'm never coming back here again. Things will change. I will change.' Yet some of them did come back, time after time. Why? Often it was because they went straight back to the environment which was the reason they were in prison in the first place. They went back to live amongst contacts who had dangerous lifestyles, taking and dealing in drugs and often without jobs or income, or any prospect of either.

Another problem was that they had no one to give them good advice when they left prison, except perhaps occasionally a probation officer or social worker. People like me were rare; someone they trusted. Many of the boys were violent when they were in prison and I would try to talk to them to vent their anger somewhere else, just as some of my teachers had tried to talk to me. There were volunteers as well who came into the prison to try to help the lads. These people acted as mentors and came to see the boys when they were in prison and also during the crucial period when they had just been released.

In my time there, I saw boys who really changed. I told them that God is not a God who walks behind us for a few years, to check how we're getting on before He decides He will be with us. The God I know comes to us straightaway, no matter what we have done or what we are doing. As long as we want Him and are deeply sorry for the things that we have done, He will be there for us.

Another big change for me at this time was my decision to go to college and obtain a qualification. I wanted to know more about the Bible and I wanted to prove people wrong; those who had told me, 'You'll always be a waste of space.' I was determined to show them that I was clever and that I could study. Eventually, I was given a place at Soundwell College to take GCSE English. It was a struggle, but I was adamant I would finish the course and my determination paid off, because I passed. That was a big day for me; the little boy who wouldn't go to school was now a model student!

I went on to take more courses that would provide me with qualifications. I passed a year-long course in counselling with a professional Christian organisation and gained a certificate in Drug Awareness Counselling. All these qualifications provided me with knowledge but perhaps more importantly, they gave me respect for myself and I felt I had the respect of those around me. How different from the young man I used to be.

By this time, Nick Hay had secured more funding and I was asked if I would like to work full-time. It was a dream come true. I would arrive in the morning, pick up the list of lads in the segregation wing and walk past the football field. I would make my way into the wing and chat to the lads there. Were they self-harming? Were they on suicide watch? There were a lot of unhappy boys in Ashfield, especially when they first arrived. These boys were frightened and I understood what that felt like.

At aged just 15 and older, a lot of the new boys were upset and missing their family. I would encourage them and say, 'Why don't you call your mum and tell her you're alright? Then you'll know she's not worrying about you.' I would often hear them crying on the phone to their mums when they thought no-one was around.

There were a load of lads who had been moved from care home to care home. One boy had been in seventy-four different placements before he arrived in prison. Another started smoking cannabis when he was 6 years old, encouraged to do so by his family, who were all drug dealers. Many of the boys had lost parents at a very early age due to drugs and many didn't know their fathers. A lot of them had close family members in prison - brothers, sisters, mums and dads. For some of the boys, both their parents were in prison when they were taken in themselves.

When you consider all of this, it is not surprising that some of these lads caused violent incidents in the prison. It was my job to 'talk them down' and I was good at it because I knew what it was like to be violent. I wish I had had someone to talk to when I was in prison. Instead, I was beaten. I was kicked to pieces and made to wash the floors in the toilets. If someone had talked to me and found out why I was being violent, I believe things would have been very different.

In Ashfield, I often spoke to the lads on suicide watch, encouraging them to take one day at a time. These were boys who had grown up with no loving dad or mum and I would try to give them hope for their future. I would encourage them to look ahead.

'Think about when you get out of here; you can go to college, you can take a few girls out and then maybe one day settle down with your own wife and children. You could be sitting down with your wife and children at Christmas and you will be able to give away that love you didn't have yourself.'

At this point, I would often find that they would open up and begin to see some hope. I never Bible-bashed. I simply told them what had happened to me. They would sometimes ask about my tattoos and scars and I would tell them I had been a criminal. After that, they always wanted to listen.

At the end of my time in the segregation wing and the hospital wing, I would go back to my office to read my emails. Throughout the day, some of the boys were booked in to talk with me and I would either meet with them in the peace and quiet of the chapel or visit them in their cells. These times were precious, when they confided in me and talked about issues in their past. Some wanted me to pray with them and they were often in tears.

A darker side of prison life was the number of deaths the boys had to cope with in their young lives. Some came from drug dealing families or families who led dangerous and violent lifestyles and many had to cope with the news whilst they were in prison of a close relative or friend who had died very young in their community.

On most days, the noticeboard in my office would read:

JB Father terminally ill

AH Go with to father's funeral

RG Brother died, go with to funeral

HS Brother Danny died, message from his mother

TH Grandmother died, message from his mother

GK Best friend murdered, message from his girlfriend

JL Girlfriend killed in crash, message from his mother

Along with the other members of the chaplaincy, it was my job to break this kind of news to the boys. When a notification of death came in; a brother or sometimes a mother or any member of the family, we had to check to make sure that the news was genuine.

This was because it was known for some families to try and get their boys out of prison by setting up false deaths, so we had to be thorough when speaking to close relatives. I had to tactfully try to find out what had really happened and then confirm it with the hospital. As soon as I was convinced the news was genuine, I would call the boy out of his classroom or cell and meet with him in the nearest private office. I tended to break the news quickly, before they even sat down. It was better that way. Then I told them we could phone their family and make arrangements for them to attend the funeral.

The boys were not permitted to attend friends' funerals. Only close relatives, a mother, father, brother or grandparent. A lot of grandparents were more like a parent to the lads and were often more involved in bringing them up than their mothers or fathers had been, so it was important they should be able to go to their funerals. There were a lot of forms which needed to be filled in, all of which were countersigned by the Prison Governor. After the forms were completed, I would liaise with the family outside and keep the boy informed as much as possible. In these circumstances, the boy was watched closely and an ACCT (Assessment, Care in Custody and Teamwork) file was opened. This notified all staff members that the lad needed special consideration and should be closely monitored. Special case conferences were held to make sure the boy was receiving the necessary support, comfort and care, including any one-to-one time, should he need it.

We were, of course, particularly kind at these times and I would often offer to accompany the boy to the funeral. If he said 'yes', I would leave the prison with the boy in handcuffs, along with two or three trained officers. I would drive to the funeral, where his handcuffs would have to be kept on. However, the officers had a way of hiding them during the funeral.

When the service was over, we would leave almost immediately and start the journey back to Ashfield. I was always glad I could be there to talk to them as we drove back. It was a very vulnerable time for the boys. It could bring up feelings of regret that they had not had a chance to say goodbye to their loved one. Sometimes they carried regret that their loved one had died knowing they were in prison. A lot of careful counselling was needed.

Once back in the prison, I would continue with my day. I held the Traveller's Group at 3.30 p.m. in the chapel. The younger ones tended to have little knowledge about their unique history and the amazing ability Gypsies had to survive in the past. I taught them about the ethnic cleansing that had taken place during the war when the Nazis murdered over 500,000 Gypsies in the death camps, alongside Jews and homosexuals. Most of the time, this was a revelation to them and it gave them pride in who they were and where they had come from. I taught them about their unique knowledge of the countryside as well and their extended, supportive family life which was rare and precious in our western culture.

After a long day of dealing with such raw emotions, I couldn't wait to get home to feed my beloved horses. Bonny and Queenie were always there to greet and nuzzle me, especially when I had something tasty for them, usually an apple, pony nuts or sugar lumps. Spending time with them and being out in the open amongst the birds and the trees was a great way for me to wind down after an emotional day. It really helped me to distance myself from the difficulties and troubles I faced at the prison.

After I had spent time with the horses, I went home to be with Sue and the kids. Then I would have my tea and sometimes after that I would go to the Empire Boxing Club to train. Another great break from the pressures of work.

Every two weeks we would attend our home group, where Sue and I continued to study the Bible and pray with others, asking God to help us in everything we did.

Life was good and it was about to get even better.

Chapter 16

BECOMING A CHAPLAIN

As time went on in Ashfield, I began to feel that I wanted to enrol on a course to learn about the Bible and the Christian faith in more depth. This, though, would be a highly academic study. I wanted to be sure I could answer all the lads' questions, some of which could be very challenging. I also wanted to learn for my own satisfaction. However, I knew it would be a huge step for me; when I was at school I really struggled with reading and writing. Would I be able to do this? I didn't know, but I wanted to try.

At least I had had some practice. As well as the English GCSE and counselling courses, I had completed a two-year Bible study course at church, which I had really enjoyed. However, studying with people I knew and with no pressure to produce any results was very different to taking an academic course amongst strangers. Nonetheless, I set my sights on Trinity College, a Church of England Theological College attached to Bristol University. I wanted to complete a two-year, part-time course, which would give me an accredited Certificate in Theology. A serious qualification.

There was just one problem; the fee was £4,000. I knew I

couldn't afford to pay for it and couldn't see any way round it, but I decided I would pray and speak to the Prison Governor and see if there was any way they could help me. Brian and the rest of the staff were good enough to recommend me and my work to Serco, the private company which ran the prison for the government. Serco amazingly agreed to pay the total cost of the course. I was over the moon.

I was on my way, but even with this support, I almost didn't make it.

Early in 2010, I had my preliminary interview. As I drove along the sweeping driveway and through the grand grounds to the college, I looked at the imposing Jacobean building. It had twisted sugar candy pillars either side of the porch and the date '1669' engraved above the doorway. Was I really going to be accepted into somewhere like this? It was far too posh for me.

I took a deep breath, put my shoulders back, pushed open the big oak door and forced myself to walk into the lobby. It was filled with people in suits and smart dresses and they all seemed to know one another. I was wearing a T-shirt and sporting multiple tattoos. I didn't belong here. Something came over me and I thought, *I really don't want to do this. I'm going.* As I turned to leave, I suddenly remembered what I used to tell the lads in the prison when they said they couldn't do anything and thought they weren't good enough.

'If there were fifty boys in university who were well-spoken, and then there were fifty boys in prison like you, who do you think God would love the most?'

Usually the lads would reply, 'Well, it's obvious, it's them.'

'That's where you're wrong,' I'd tell them. 'God loves you just as much as He loves those boys in the university. He wants you to have a better life and He doesn't love them better than He loves you.'

With my own words ringing in my ears, I turned back, looked at the crowd of students and decided I was going to stay.

This was the start of a challenging two years for everyone on the course, not just for me, but for my fellow students and the professors! I wasn't afraid to speak out and I often voiced the unspoken thoughts of others in the room, especially when there was a particularly highbrow philosophical point that I felt just wasn't practical. I would speak up and challenge the lecturer when the other students would hold back, afraid they would embarrass themselves. I particularly struggled when I was presented with new ideas that went against what I believed and had experienced for myself. Because of all these things, the course was one of the hardest things I had ever had to do.

In addition to this, I had recently been diagnosed as dyslexic, so I had problems with reading and writing. I thought it was a shame that I hadn't been diagnosed when I was little, while struggling at school. It may sound strange, but it was a great relief for me to find out I was dyslexic. I finally realized that I didn't find it difficult to read because I was stupid, but because I had dyslexia.

My newly diagnosed condition meant that I was given a new laptop, a Dictaphone and a printer to help me with taking notes and writing essays. These were a huge help to me, but even better than that, I was given two hours a week to study with a helper called Chris. Chris was employed to come into the prison one evening a week after work. He sat with me and we talked through the notes from that week, then he helped me to organise my essays. He was brilliant; he wasn't ever stressed or angry with me. I was very grateful to Chris and to everyone else who helped me through my studies.

But it was an exhausting regime.

Tuesday nights were spent at the college. I would go straight after work emotionally drained with the baggage of prison life. In addition to this, I had to use any spare hours I had to study. But I was determined to stick it out. Each night after feeding the horses, I would go home and study.

My knowledge grew and grew. I learned more about the Bible and the beginnings of Christianity, its history right up to the present day. I found it all fascinating. Sometimes, when it got too academic, I found it frustrating. Despite that, I kept going and two years later I left the college the proud owner of an accredited Certificate in Theology.

Sue and the kids were so proud of me.

I was thrilled to have got the qualification, but God clearly had other things in mind when He had prompted me to complete that course. Because just a year after I qualified at Trinity College, the government announced that all prison chaplains had to be licensed and ordained. I panicked. I wasn't licensed or ordained. I thought I was going to lose my job, but I didn't. Why? My certificate saved me. The only reason I was considered to be ordained and licenced was because I held that Certificate in Theology.

I had to travel to London to be interviewed by my church leaders before the Churches in the Community would accept and licence me. I was nervous at first but, dressed in my best suit, I braced myself as I walked into the room. I quickly relaxed and found I enjoyed chatting with them and having the opportunity to tell them my story. My interviewer, Trevor Howard, enjoyed it too. My story was so different from the usual folk who applied for licence ordination that my interview lasted two-and-a-half hours instead of the one I had been allocated.

Despite my unusual background, or perhaps because of it, and due to my faith and perseverance, I was accepted to become ordained. I was going to be a trained member of the clergy with the authority to lead services, preach and baptize people.

My Ordination Service was a great event. It was held in my own church, and my family, friends and many of my colleagues from the prison came to watch. They joined in with the laughter, the happy tears and the clapping as the representatives from Churches in the Community made their speeches and I was finally handed my certificate. I stood and smiled, taking in the congratulations of everyone around me.

It was such a happy occasion.

I was really proud of what I had achieved. I had gone from barely being able to read and write, to studying at university. I had once been one of the most notorious troublemakers in my area and now I was an ordained member of the church! In fact, it was such an unusual achievement that at the next annual conference of Churches in the Community, Trevor introduced me to all the people there:

'Before people come up for an interview, we have to ask them if they have any previous convictions. Larry arrived with a long list of them. So many, in fact, that they went on for several pages! We looked through them all and then asked Larry, "What happened after all of these convictions?" He replied straightaway in his wonderful Bristolian accent, "I got saved!'"

Everyone at the conference laughed and afterwards many congratulated me.

I was ready for the next step on my journey.

Chapter 17

NO TIME LIKE THE PRESENT

For four years a Christian charity called *Friends on the Out* had been run from within the Young Offenders chaplaincy. FOTO aimed to recruit volunteers from local churches to help the lads find work and not reoffend once they left Ashfield. The Trustees had recently appointed someone new to run it, Hilary, who had previously worked for *Tearfund* and the BBC.

I had to work closely with her and was asked if I minded sharing my small office with her. I agreed. The office, with the two of us in it, was so small that if anyone wanted to come out of the chapel into the admin corridor, Hilary had to get out of her chair and stand up to allow them the space to open the chapel door.

Shortly after she arrived and whilst I was away on holiday, it was announced that all the offices were to be repainted and the person in the office could choose any colour they wanted. Hilary chose a rather fetching, feminine shade of lilac for the walls, totally forgetting that I would have to live with the colour too. The office was duly painted and it did look very nice, if a little out of place for a YOI! When I returned from my holiday, I unlocked my office door and reeled back in shock. What had happened to my domain?!

When Hilary arrived several hours later, I barely managed to contain myself.

'What happened to the office?'

'Oh', said Hilary happily. 'It's nice, isn't it?'

I never quite got over the shock of my lilac office. We laughed about it when she had realised what she'd done. Ironically, she was soon moved into her own office opposite mine and this meant that the colour of her new office was a dull cream which she hated! Meanwhile, I was stuck in my delicate lilac room, which I hated just as passionately. Although I did get used to it eventually and even, reluctantly, admitted that I quite liked it!

These were good days in the prison and Hilary decided she needed an assistant and mentioned this to me. In spite of the lilac office incident she and I had become good friends and I suggested Sue might be a good candidate. Hilary prayed about it and felt strongly that she should meet Sue. They got on really well and Sue happily accepted the twelve hours a week that the charity could afford. Both were delighted and a lifelong friendship was born from that happy appointment.

Sue settled quickly into the work and the lads really liked her. It was great having her around. She was able to talk to the boys about their lives and totally empathize with them. She and Hilary would set out together from their little office to visit the boys in the cell blocks. It was a wonderful time but it could be emotionally draining as well. The boys were often hard to get through to but Sue, Hilary and myself met with the rest of the chaplaincy team each morning to pray together, asking God to give us the right words for the boys we were going to visit that day. And for the first time in prison history, staff members were recruited as mentors to the lads as well as outside volunteers.

The second big change was not such a happy one. Nick Hay, the Head of the Chaplaincy, decided it was time for him to leave. He had been at Ashfield for ten years and had built a solid relationship with the boys, his chaplaincy staff and the rest of the staff within the prison. He was highly respected and would be sorely missed. With great sadness, myself and the rest of the chaplaincy staff said goodbye to a caring, kind and hardworking colleague.

I continued to work long hours in the chaplaincy. Boys came and went. As always, some responded more to help than others. It was tough dealing with their broken lives, getting to the heart of how they really felt and trying to be a reliable father figure to them. Many had never known a stable family life.

Lots of the boys would write to me after they left and I kept in touch with them. Too often though, I didn't need to write to them because they would be back in prison not long after they had been released. When they were out of prison, most had no alternative but to go back to their old way of life; often with no job, no stable home, too many temptations and very little help. It was just too hard for them to change their lives around completely. Once they were back inside, they could confide in me or the other members of the chaplaincy. They could share their real feelings of loneliness, despair and anger; it was a vital outlet for them. I cared deeply for them and I tried to show them that I understood.

The years went by until there was some difficult news. The

government asked Serco to close Ashfield as a YOI and reopen it as a sex offenders' prison. This was a big shock for the staff who worked there. Ashfield YOI seemed to be a particularly well-run institute. It had its problems as all prisons do, but most of the staff were second to none in their care and concern for the young lads. The experience and knowledge they had built up in all departments, the education department particularly, would be hard to replace. The lads would be scattered to young offenders' sections within adult prisons across the country, far away from friends and family in a lot of cases. Many of the dedicated and trained staff members lost their jobs. It was not a happy time. I was one of those who suffered as a result. The chaplaincy staff numbers had to be reduced and I was told I was one of those who had to leave.

I was heartbroken. It had always seemed to me that I was meant to work with these young boys and I knew that I made a difference in their lives, but there was no going back. The boys were scattered. There was no specialist unit for me to work in. Perhaps God had other plans for me. Where would I go now? How would I earn a living? Sue and I prayed on our knees for many hours and days but there didn't seem to be anywhere for us to turn.

Then one day I was told of a part-time vacancy in Horfield Prison, Bristol. Horfield was an old, worn-out adult prison, bizarrely set in the middle of a housing suburb in Bristol. I applied, went for an interview and was given the job. I was so relieved. Even though it was only part-time and I would be working with adults and not the young teenagers to whom I felt I could relate. However, I knew God must have a reason for me to be there and that's what I told myself on the first day of my new job.

I walked in through the foreboding entrance to the prison, its huge red, Victorian brick walls closing me in. It was an ominous building and one I remembered only too well from my past. At least this time I was here because I wanted to be, not because I had been arrested and forced to stay. I was now working in the prison in which I had been a prisoner!

I collected my keys and was taken up to my office. It was a Portakabin which I would share with the head chaplain and other part-time clergy. There were leaflets, books and coffee cups scattered over the two desks and chairs. This was to be home for me for many years to come.

After my orientation course and introductions to work colleagues, I left the office and set off to look around my new place of service. Being there brought back so many memories of my time as a prisoner in one of its cells. The helplessness of being shut in. Now I was the one with the keys. I could walk out of there that evening and every evening. The men could not. I wondered how it would feel for me to visit them in their cells or speak to them in the chapel where I had sat and not understood the preacher.

It would be a new experience for me to be able to walk across those courtyards a free man. I remembered distinctly the massive metal clanging gate and the huge bins backed against the tall wire fences. I remembered stepping over the occasional dead rat and entering the clamour of the old and worn-out cellblocks. The prison was just as I remembered, but I was totally different. Now, I had the freedom to come and go and more importantly, I had the freedom to talk to the men and tell them about God's love and special care for them.

It wasn't long before I found that God had something else for me too. Not long after I arrived, a post for a full-time chaplain came up. This was a rare opportunity and I wasn't about to waste it. As I prepared for the interview, I practised and practised what I was going to say and ran through mock scenarios and questions. With all my experiences, there was hardly anything I had not had to face or deal with, almost on a daily basis. Thankfully, my preparation paid off. The interview went well and out of a lot of candidates, I was appointed full-time chaplain.

This was a huge step for me. It meant I could put my experience and common sense to good use in dealing with the many troubled men in the prison. It was more difficult than dealing with the young lads in the YOI, but it was where God wanted me to be.

Although it was tough, I enjoyed talking to the men. They told me breath-taking stories of hardship and violence. The conditions in the prison were far from perfect; it was overcrowded, and the buildings were old and worn out. It could be a depressing place to work but my colleagues kept each other going and there were often breakthroughs with the men during conversations in their cells or in chapel that were encouraging.

After a while, I was added to the rota to lead two morning services in the chapel on Sundays. Each time, I would stand in front of the men and look at their sad faces. Some had been in prison for years and others, much younger, had only just arrived. I always began with my story.

'Yes, I've been where you are now. I've been in more fights than you'll ever know. I've taken a lot of illegal drugs and yes, drugs are great, at first. Otherwise, why would we all take them?'

At this point, the prisoners would sit up and begin to listen. They had never heard anything like this before, let alone from a chaplain in a church. Then I would continue:

'But do you know what drugs do to you? They destroy your life, completely.'

Then I would share my story of how I started smoking cannabis at a young age and how it would give me the giggles, but as the years went by and I became dependent, I started to have mood swings and ended up feeling depressed and angry.

'Cannabis led me to take harder drugs. Eventually, drugs make you miserable and can make you turn to crime. They take over your life. Ultimately, they may be the reason you have ended up in here, either for a long period of time or sometimes for the rest of your life.'

Now, the younger men would really be listening to me.

'My life has completely changed. I now know that there is a God and that He knows each and every one of us, no matter what we have done. He knows us so well that He will guide our lives if we ask Him to. If we really, really want to change, we can. I am living proof of His love and care.'

I would then continue to share with them about what God had done in my life.

Each time, there would be silence in the pews as I told them about the amazing twists and turns in my journey. I would speak of how God was with me, even when I didn't realize it. He was there at every turn.

I always ended the service by asking if anyone wanted to come and speak with me. There were always men who wanted to have a chat; they were often amazed at how my life had been turned around and they wanted God to do the same thing in their lives too. With the grace of God, I would help them to realize that Jesus could be their friend and brother through it all, no matter what they had done or how hopeless their lives appeared.

'God is everywhere, not only in that chapel. He was and is in the prison as well as outside the gates'. I used to tell the men.

'Jesus is not just outside the gate waiting for you to be released. He won't walk behind you for the next few years to see how you're doing. He is here right now, 24/7. He doesn't work shifts. No matter who you are, what you have done or where you have come from, Jesus loves you and He will give you another chance. It happened to me, it can happen to you.'

A PRAYER TO START AGAIN

If you would like to start your life afresh, you can pray the following prayer to say sorry to God:

> Lord Jesus,
> I am sorry for all the wrong things I have done in my life
> I ask you to forgive me
> I believe you died on the cross for me
> And that you rose again in three days
> I ask you to come into my life
> As my Lord, my Saviour
> And my best friend
> Amen.

You may feel after reading this book that you don't really need God in your life because you have never been in any trouble, or been in prison, and you've actually lived a reasonably honest life.

However, the Bible tells us that we have *all* sinned and fallen short of the glory of God (Romans 3:23).

The truth is, we all need to repent and start afresh.

There's no time like the present.

If you would like to talk to someone about having another chance with God, or would like someone to pray with you, you can email me at: larrysueharvey@btinternet.com

You can also go to your local Christian church fellowship and speak to the pastor or vicar and ask them to pray with you.

UPDATE

- Larry Harvey still serves full time as a Prison Chaplain and is now also a trained Family Liaison Officer, going with the Governor to break the bad news of a death in Custody to the family and supporting them in any way he can.

- He is a trained ACCT Assessor and visits prisoners on suicide watch who must be assessed after 24 hours to check if they are still at risk.

- He is part of the Care Team and keeps a prison mobile phone outside of office hours so that staff can call him if they need to.

- Larry came 2nd in the Southwest Regional Awards for his work at HMP Bristol.

- He still meets up with between thirty and forty of his old mates from the Empire Sports Club every six weeks for a meal.

- Joanne went in and out of hospital over the years for smaller operations and is doing well. She has a little girl of her own now and is very close to God.

- Sue and Larry have five children and six grandchildren, all very much loved.

- They still have contact with Professor Bolger and are eternally grateful to him for all that he did for Joanne and their family.

- They attend church regularly and are truly thankful to God for all He has done in their lives.

KNIFE CRIME AND DRUGS

A Message from Larry

There is a lot of knife crime around.

If you have a problem with someone or you just carry a knife for your own protection, the chances are, at some point, it will be used. The end result could be you taking a person's life.

That dead person's family would be devastated and never get over it.

Your family would also be devastated, because you would be in prison for a minimum of 20 years or more. The best days of your life would be thrown away.

If you are going to open that kitchen drawer and look at that knife, then think of the consequences and close the drawer and leave the knife where it is. If you don't carry one, you can't use it!

We all have one life on this earth - why spend it in prison!

If you are still at school and maybe your mates are taking drugs and maybe you feel you need to do the same so that you can fit in, just be strong - you don't have to do what someone else does just to fit in.

Make your own decisions. Believe me, they will respect you at some point because you said "NO".

The end result of taking illegal drugs into your 20's and 30's is that you will most likely have mental health issues, depression and other serious problems.

The job of illegal drugs and the abuse of alcohol is to destroy your life. There are no happy families when you get involved in this. It is never too late to change your life and come away from drugs and/or alcohol.

Before I became a Christian, if I was in a situation where I had a problem, or I was stressed, I would go to the pub and get drunk or take drugs. Now if something stressful crops up I get on my knees and hand it over to God.

If you are tempted with using a knife, or taking drugs to fit in with your mates, think again. Speak to someone you trust to help you. Or you can email me on: larrysueharvey@btinternet.com

SOUTHMEAD HOSPITAL CHARITY

Thanks to our fundraisers and donors we support projects which really improve the care our patients at North Bristol NHS Trust (NBT) receive and projects which help develop our staff.

We raise funds for Southmead Hospital in Bristol, Cossham Hospital and community health services in Bristol, South Gloucestershire and North Somerset. Our aim is to make life better for the 500,000 patients our Trust treat every year and for our staff by funding:

- medical research
- specialist equipment
- patient and staff support
- improvements to the hospital environment

All of the projects we support are beyond the remit of the NHS but really enrich the healthcare we provide.

All profits collected from this book sale will support the Neurosurgery Department at Southmead Hospital Bristol

Find out more about us:

southmeadhospitalcharity.org.uk

Disclaimer: The views and opinions expressed in this book are solely of Larry Harvey and do not express the views of opinions of North Bristol NHS Trust or Southmead Hospital Charity

Follow us on

Larry's Mum and Dad travelling in the 60's

Mum, brother Pete on left, Larry by pram

Larry on right. Pete. Mum

Far left brother George. b-in-law Scutty. sister Kathy. brother Joe. Mum. on Mum's lap brother Pete and Larry. far right Dad.

Far left brother Pete. Larry. brother Joe. nephew Henry.
and far right brother George

Dad's Rolls Royce: Larry far left. Joe. Dad. George. Little Joe. Joe's son

Empire Sports Club: Larry aged 14 centre. Pete front far right

Larry aged 15 years

1979 Bridgwater Fayre Boxing Booth

1979 Bridgwater Fayre: Larry Winning at the Boxing Booth

Cross. Chapel Frenchay Hospital where Larry prayed

Larry. Sue. Joanne. Professor Ceiran Bolger

2000. Larry being Baptised

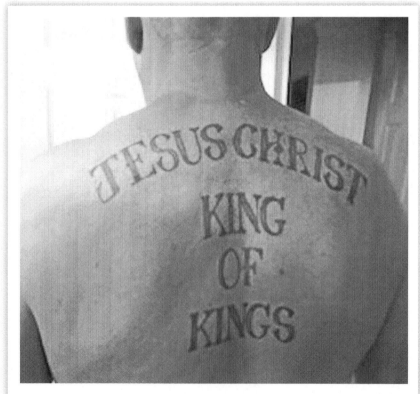

New Tattoo!

Larry and Sue

2001. one of many missionary trips to Ukraine

2016. Larry with his horse & cart

2016. Larry's pet horses

2016. Larry's pet horses

2017. Larry's home

Larry outside one of his caravans for travelling

Printed in Great Britain
by Amazon